THE
NAZIS'
FLIGHT FROM
JUSTICE

THE NAZIS'
FLIGHT FROM
JUSTICE

HOW HITLER'S FOLLOWERS ATTEMPTED TO VANISH WITHOUT TRACE

RICHARD DARGIE AND JULIAN FLANDERS

This edition published in 2021 by Arcturus Publishing Limited
26/27 Bickels Yard, 151–153 Bermondsey Street,
London SE1 3HA

AD006653UK

Printed in the UK

CONTENTS

INTRODUCTION

THE NAME Adolf Hitler is synonymous with one of the deadliest and most destructive conflicts in history, which claimed the lives of more than 50 million people, including an estimated six million Jews murdered through systematic genocide. Little is known with certainty about how a son born to Klara and Alois Hitler on 20 April 1889, on a dull, grey Easter Saturday, would turn into one of the world's most tyrannical and murderous dictators, but there is no doubt that World War II was Hitler's war.

Hitler's plans to establish a thousand-year Aryan Third Reich were put into action soon after his appointment as chancellor of Germany by President Hindenburg on 30 January 1933. Swiftly consolidating power, he appointed himself Führer (supreme leader) in 1934, and the path to war became clear. Rearmament began in the mid-1930s in advance of his sending troops into Austria in 1938 and Czechoslovakia the following year. In August 1939, Hitler and Joseph Stalin signed the German–Soviet Non-aggression Pact, and on 1 September Germany invaded Poland from the west with Soviet help from the east. Two days later, Britain and France declared war on Germany.

Of course, Hitler did not act alone. He had taken power by diplomatic means, and his views generated enormous and genuine support among not only the powerful German officer class but also among millions of everyday citizens who voted for the Nazi Party. By pulling together strands of right-wing thinking already present in Germany, Hitler increased his popularity irresistibly. For many historians, the key to his success was his charisma, best illustrated through the inspirational power of his speeches, which often left his audience spellbound. According to eyewitness Konrad Heiden, 'His speeches are daydreams of this mass soul... The speeches always begin with deep pessimism and end in overjoyed redemption, a triumphant happy ending; often they can be refuted by reason, but they follow the far mightier logic of the subconscious, which no refutation can touch... Hitler has given speech to the speechless terror of the modern mass...'

This is a view confirmed by Sir Nevile Henderson, British ambassador to Berlin in the 1930s, who said, 'Hitler owed his success in the struggle for power to the fact that he was the reflection of their [his supporters'] subconscious mind, and his ability to express in words what that subconscious mind felt that it wanted.'

Through these speeches, Hitler sold a simple message to the German public, offering national redemption and the promise of a new Germany with him as its supreme leader. In return, he demanded that all citizens would serve the state. Democracy and individual rights would be sacrificed for the good of the nation. Dissent would not be tolerated. Following the Great Depression – the world economic crisis that followed the Wall Street Crash in 1929 – the German economy dipped into recession, further undermining the government. The people's faith in capitalism and democracy was evaporating. Hitler's dream of a New Order – putting Germany first, with strong leadership and an end to economic ills – quickly became the people's dream. They flocked to join the Nazi Party, the Hitler Youth, the League of German Girls and other organizations that made up the new *Volksgemeinschaft* (national community). In this way, the Nazi message sent deep roots down through every level of society.

Of course, propaganda played a major part in this. For historian Karl Bracher, the success of Nazi ideology can only really be understood through its use of the media and culture. He points to the use of modern techniques of opinion-formation to create a 'truly religio-psychological phenomenon' that made it so powerful.

When the fighting stopped, in early May 1945, it was as though the lights had gone out, as though National Socialism – a political movement that had attracted broader support than any other in Germany, and had inspired six years of war across the globe – had disappeared. As if waking from a nightmare, the German population, exhausted by the violence and relieved that war was finally over, reacted as if Hitler and the Nazis already belonged to a distant past. Uniforms were discarded, portraits of Hitler were taken down and destroyed. As historian Richard Bessel put it in his book *Germany 1945: From War to Peace*, 'Coming on top of the shock of the extreme violence during the previous months, the grotesque, bloody end of the Third Reich completely undermined its legitimacy and popular support for Nazism.'

In the aftermath of any war, there are more questions than answers. *The Nazis' Flight from Justice* examines those questions that arose in 1945. How did the son of an Austrian customs officer from Braunau am Inn became the self-proclaimed saviour of Germany, give birth to a political party that, at its height, boasted at least eight million members and led an 18 million-strong army into a war for world domination? How did this man, described as 'an empty vessel' by historian Ian Kershaw, have such an immense historical impact? How did he persuade ordinary citizens to perpetrate systematic war crimes, massacres, mass rapes, looting, the extermination of forced labour and POWs and the genocidal killing of European Jews, many of whom died in the 44,000 Nazi camps? The book also examines what happened to those Nazis who survived the war, particularly the many thousands implicated in war crimes. Who was to be held responsible? Where was justice to be found? How were the punishments made to fit the crimes? Where did all the Nazis go?

With the end of World War II now over 75 years ago, any Nazis remaining on the wanted lists will be in their 90s. The book ends by examining the most significant trials of the post-war era as Germany fast approaches the moment where there will be no individuals left to prosecute for the crimes of the Holocaust.

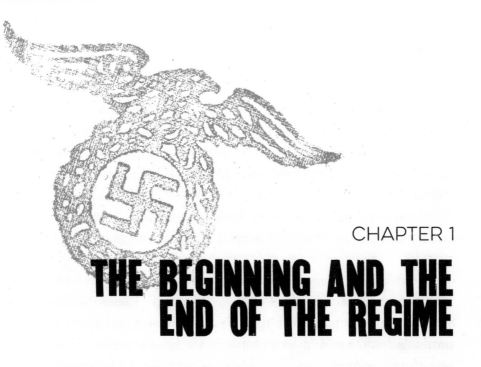

THE BEGINNING AND THE END OF THE REGIME

FOUND GUILTY of high treason for his part in planning to topple the Weimar Republic by revolution in November 1923, Adolf Hitler, leader of the National Socialist German Workers' Party – Nazi for short – was sent to prison for five years. On the night of 8 November, Nazi stormtroopers attempted to take over several government buildings while Hitler gave a table-top speech in Munich's Bürgerbräukeller to a crowd of some 3,000 people announcing a national revolution and the formation of a new government. Despite his rowdy and generally supportive audience, the plan broke down because of a lack of organization and the evening ended in chaos.

The following day, determined to save face, the putschists marched through the centre of the city towards the war ministry building. En route they were stopped by a police cordon. A fierce gun battle ensued leaving 18 dead and others, including Hermann Göring, injured. Hitler was arrested and charged with treason. Although the Beer Hall Putsch, as it was known, was a failure in that there was no widespread uprising, the attendant publicity meant that the party took a great leap forward. The trial that followed created sensational headlines and garnered much support for the new party. Hitler even impressed the trial judges, who handed down a very lenient sentence for such a serious crime.

In the event, Hitler served only 13 months in the relative luxury of Landsberg prison near Munich. He was allowed to stroll in its grounds, receive regular visitors and make use of its extensive library. He later described his time there as 'free education at the state's expense'. As well as reading, his business manager suggested that he used the time to produce an autobiography. Lacking confidence in his writing, Hitler only agreed when offered the services of a ghost-writer, a job taken up by his friend and fellow party member Rudolf Hess, who was also in prison for taking part in the putsch. The resulting book, *Mein Kampf* ('My Struggle'), outlined his political manifesto.

Developing themes from the party's Twenty-Five Point Programme for the rebuilding of the country, published in 1920, which stressed the importance of the abolition of the Treaty of Versailles, the nationalization of large businesses and industries, strong central government, the purity of the German race and generous old-age pensions, *Mein Kampf* is a difficult read. Unlike the speeches for which Hitler had already gained a reputation, the text was boring, repetitive and hard to understand. However, it set out the main beliefs he had for the Nazi Party: a belief in National Socialism that included the importance of racial purity and state control of the economy; Aryans as the 'master race', superior to all others and, in particular, Jews and communists; war and struggle as an essential part of Aryan life; *Lebensraum* ('Living space') gained from expansion into Russia and Poland and finally strength

Returning hero: released from Landsberg prison in 1924, where he had been jailed for his part in the Beer Hall Putsch, Hitler embarks on a triumphant tour of Munich.

from total loyalty to its leader – the Führer. Hitler wrote, 'A stronger race will drive out the weaker ones, for the vital urge in its ultimate form will break down the absurd barriers of the so-called humanity of individuals to make way for the humanity of Nature, which destroys the weak to give their place to the strong.' It was nothing less than the law of the jungle.

STABBED IN THE BACK

On 9 November 1918, with Germany on the verge of defeat at the end of World War I, Kaiser Wilhelm II, emperor of Germany and commander-in-chief of the German armed forces, abdicated under pressure from US president Woodrow Wilson and fled across the border into Holland, bringing an end to the Second Reich. After four years of war and millions of deaths, troops and supplies were exhausted. With significant disillusionment and unrest in the country, and with the monarchy dissolved, Berlin was paralysed by a general strike. There was revolution in the air. Keen to negotiate the best possible peace terms with President Wilson and the Allies, generals Ludendorff and Hindenburg, who had led the country throughout the conflict, handed the reins of power over to the left-leaning Social Democrats, giving them the job of forming a democracy, the system favoured by the victors. On 9 November, a republic was proclaimed.

In the ferment that followed during the last weeks of 1918 and early 1919, there was a maelstrom of extremist political demonstrations across the country on both the right and left of the spectrum, in particular by the communist Spartacists led by Rosa Luxemburg. The movement was crushed in January and later that month elections put a liberal government in place. On 7 May, however, came a hammer blow to the 'new' Germany when the terms of the Treaty of Versailles were published.

Although 30 nations were represented in discussions at the Paris Peace Conference, the terms were really agreed between France, Britain and the US. Naturally, Clémenceau, Lloyd George and Wilson each approached the talks from the point of view of their own self-interest: Clémenceau desired to punish Germany and ensure it was too weak to attack France again; Lloyd George wanted punishment but insurance that Germany was strong enough to trade; while Wilson was keen to ensure that Germany was not destroyed and stated his aim of creating a League of Nations to keep peace in the future. In the event, no one was really happy with the agreement and the terms were punitive: Germany was asked to accept the blame for starting the war, it was to pay £6.6 billion in reparations, its borders were changed and its overseas territories were taken by France and Britain. In addition, the German army was reduced to 100,000 volunteers only, the air force was disbanded completely and the navy reduced to six battleships, while the Rhineland – the border area between Germany and France – was demilitarized. On top of this, Germany was not allowed to join the League of Nations until it had proved its peaceful intentions.

There were howls of outrage from all corners of Germany and the other defeated nations, and also from France who thought the terms not harsh enough, and from Britain where some felt they were too harsh. However, facing the possibility of a new Allied invasion if they failed to agree to it, the German government signed the treaty at the Palace of Versailles on 28 June 1919. The first job faced by the newly named Weimar Republic, following the publication of its constitution in July, was to address the fallout from military defeat, a collapsed economy and a nation divided over its future, with many citizens failing to accept either the peace treaty or the republic itself.

One fierce critic of defeat and the terms of the treaty, a decorated war hero and passionate German nationalist despite being an Austrian citizen, was the 30-year-old Adolf Hitler. Angry and shocked by the German surrender the previous year, he believed the army had not been defeated on the battlefield but had been 'stabbed in the back' by civilian leaders, by Jews as war-profiteers and shirkers who had avoided service on the front lines, and by Marxists who had then agreed to the intolerable peace terms. Having fought in the conflict himself, been wounded twice and decorated for his bravery, Hitler decided that his future lay in politics.

BIRTH OF THE NAZI PARTY

By this time, Hitler was living in Munich, which was also consumed with revolutionary activity. The city witnessed a short-lived socialist 'people's republic' (the Räterepublic) set up by the workers and crushed on behalf of the government by the right-wing paramilitary *Freikorps* in May 1919. Still in the army, at this point employed as an intelligence officer, Hitler was able to give information about those involved in setting up the workers' revolt. His input was appreciated and he was nominated to serve on a committee to monitor the political scene in a city described by historian Ian Kershaw as 'crammed with barricades, barbed-wire and army control-points'. On 12 September, as part of his work, he was sent to a meeting of the German Workers' Party at the city's Sterneckerbräu, which was a brewery with an inn attached to it.

Anton Drexler's aim when he set up the party earlier that year was to establish a workers' party that was strongly nationalistic. Some members espoused hate for the newly established republic, vowing to destroy it, while others called for the elimination of the Jews and the recognition of Aryan superiority. Liking what he heard, Hitler soon enrolled in the far-right party, delighted to meet others who were anti-Semitic, anti-capitalist, anti-Marxist and nationalist.

Drexler was immediately impressed with the energy and can-do attitude of his new recruit. As party meetings drew larger audiences and new members, Hitler was given responsibility for developing the party's political aims and its methods of propaganda. On 24 February 1920, he gave his most effective speech yet at the city-centre Hofbräuhaus in which he outlined the party's 25-point manifesto. Having found his voice, his audience and his subject, his speeches had begun to tap into the latent fear, frustration, resentment and anger felt by many Germans at that point. Using his own anger and the hatred he directed at those he accused of causing Germany's problems, his points were cheered by the raucous, beered-up crowd. His was not a new message, nor was it unique to his party, but with his developing skills as an orator, he was able to maximize the effect of his words. Two months later, the party was renamed the National Socialist German Workers' Party. Meetings were well attended, raucous and liable to cause trouble because Hitler's speeches stirred up nationalist passions. Enraged political opponents tried to disrupt them. To deal with the resulting security issues, Hitler formed the *Sturmabteilung* (SA), brown-shirted thugs, as protection. Within a year, Hitler had replaced Drexler as party leader.

POLITICAL UPS AND DOWNS

Meanwhile, the Weimar Republic staggered on. In 1923, following the appointment of Gustav Stresemann as chancellor, Germany achieved a measure of political stability in the form of a coalition of moderate parties that won the 1924 and 1928 elections. The economy benefitted from huge loans and investment from the US, and from an agreement to extend the period of repayment of reparations imposed at Versailles. Jobs were created to rebuild the country with new technology, housing and public works such as sports stadiums and swimming pools; production levels rose, as did exports, wages and welfare payments. In 1926, following guarantees that Germany would not attempt to change its borders with France and Belgium, it was accepted into the League of Nations. Culture also underwent a renaissance, particularly in Berlin where writers, poets and filmmakers flourished and where the night-life was vibrant.

The revival was fragile, however, and consequently so was the nascent democracy. Although the coalition held together, there were 11 chancellors in the decade following the war as Germans remained unsure whether politicians were working for the people or for themselves. The economic boom worked for some and not others, with steel and chemical industries, big businesses – many of them owned by Jews – and landowners benefitting more than peasant farmers and the middle classes. There was also the possibility that the US loans could be called in at any time. This led to a backlash among the rural population against the perceived moral decline in the cultural life of Berlin and other cities. People also criticized Stresemann for agreeing to join the League of Nations, seeing it as meaning that Germany accepted the Treaty of Versailles. Trouble continued to brew.

The Nazis remained a minority party in the first few years of the 1920s, although Hitler made full use of his skills as an orator and rabble-rouser to stir the nationalist pot and make as much 'noise' as possible. His messages were consistent and simple: he promised to make Germany great again after the humiliation of World War I through strong leadership; he also promised jobs, homes, security and honour – 'work, freedom and bread'.

During 1924, with Hitler in prison, the mish-mash of right-wing politicians and parties in Germany indulged in squabbles and arguments on political tactics, strategy and ideology, coming across to the public as disunited racists and extremists on the edges of the political spectrum. Results for the Reichstag elections in December that year illustrated a huge decline in support for the Right. This was manna from heaven for Hitler. It gave him an opportunity. As well as setting out his beliefs in *Mein Kampf*, he used his time in prison to plan his route to power by democratic means. Taking cues from the other extremist parties, particularly the communists, he began to organize small local branches of the party and youth organizations of like-minded supporters. He expanded the SA, selecting his most fanatical supporters, many of them former soldiers, to join the newly formed SS (*Schutzstaffel*) and the Hitler Youth. Despite their expanding membership, the Nazis won only 12 seats in the 1928 elections.

Thanks to continuing criticism of the republic, particularly accusations that it only helped the rich, Hitler's message was increasingly effective. He began to point the way forward, blaming Jews and communists for the country's problems and claiming that, unlike the weak republican government, he was prepared to make the harsh decisions needed to turn things around. The Nazi machine was becoming more sophisticated, and it began to target those who were not benefitting from the republic's economic policies: peasant farmers, shopkeepers and other small business owners and the large rural population of the country (some 35 per cent of its inhabitants) most of whom saw themselves as racially pure Germans, fed up with competition from Jewish businesses and hearing stories of corruption, crime and immorality in the nation's cities.

The Nazi Party served up a heady cocktail of promises for the future, with guaranteed membership of the 'master race'. Delivered with confidence and strength, the Nazi message saw membership of the party climb to 100,000 in 1928. Later that year, Joseph Goebbels, one of Hitler's most fervent admirers, was appointed head of Nazi propaganda. He modernized the party's campaign methods, creating populist slogans, posters and pamphlets that appealed to people's feelings. He also used radio broadcasts, film and staged rallies in a radical new way to get Hitler's messages across.

THE GREAT DEPRESSION

In October 1929, disaster struck for the republic when Stresemann died, and for the world economy in the wake of the Wall Street Crash. The economic effects of the Great Depression that followed were felt all over the world, but Germany was particularly badly affected. Its banks were asked to return the money they had borrowed from the US for the post-war recovery. Economic collapse was not slow in following as more and more businesses went bankrupt, workers were laid off and unemployment soared. During the winters of 1930–31 and 1931–32, over six million Germans were unemployed, meaning statistically that in one of every two families the breadwinner was out of work.

With Stresemann gone, so too was the glue that held the republic together. The democratic parties could not agree on the policies needed to get the country back to work. The Nazi message of strong leadership, disobeying the rules set by the

Treaty of Versailles and tackling the problems of unemployment came into sharp focus for many Germans. The Nazis won 107 seats in the 1930 elections and 230 in 1932, making them the single biggest party in the Reichstag.

Goebbels ramped up his efforts, creating posters with campaigning slogans rather than definite policies, appealing to people's emotions rather than their brains. Goebbels explained his methods: 'There are two ways to make a revolution. You can blast your enemy with machine guns until he acknowledges the superiority of those holding the machine guns. That is one way. Or you can transform the nation through a revolution of the spirit...'

The Nazis also hammered away at those whom they felt were to blame for Germany's problems, the republic, the Jews, the communists and the Treaty of Versailles. They had read the public mood correctly, something underlined by their leader's brand of charismatic nationalism. He was to lead the country back to work, calling on the unemployed to join the army, manufacture armaments and build roads – Hitler later used the opening of the world's first motorway in 1933 as an example of what could be done by a disciplined workforce under state control. He toured the country by plane, giving all the appearances of a dynamic leader and a man of the people who understood his country.

Of course, not everyone supported the Nazis, but many of those sceptical of Hitler and his motives shared their fears: of communists, of Jews and of the politicians and policies of the Weimar Republic. The political situation was dire and there were three elections in 1932, during which time the German parliament met only five times. In March, Hitler stood in the presidential election, coming second to the incumbent Paul von

Hindenburg. Hitler demanded to be made chancellor but was refused. In January 1933, however, Hindenburg realized that to get his policies through he needed someone in the post who had support in the Reichstag, and appointed Hitler as chancellor.

THE NAZIS TAKE POWER

From the very first moment Hitler took power, he and the Nazi Party began to execute the plan that he had set out in *Mein Kampf*. At this point, Germany was in uproar with speeches, rallies, demonstrations and street fighting in many of its major cities. Hitler called another election in March and the Nazi propaganda machine moved into overdrive, with the additional advantages of now holding power over the opposition press, much of which was shut down, and control of the streets either via the police or the SA. A few days before the election, the Reichstag building was set on fire. Hitler was quick to blame the communists, claiming this was the beginning of an uprising. He demanded emergency powers to deal with this and Hindenburg acquiesced. Arrests followed swiftly; some 4,000 communists along with other Nazi opponents were taken off the streets.

The election saw the Nazis win their biggest-ever share of the vote – 43.9 per cent – which secured an absolute majority of 52 per cent due to their coalition with the Nationalist Party. Hitler immediately banned the Communist Party and engineered the passing of the Enabling Act, giving his cabinet full legislative powers without the president's involvement, for four years. This effectively made him dictator. Within weeks, he had cleared the civil service, court and educational systems of 'alien elements', including Jews and other Nazi critics, banned all trade unions, passed a law preventing the formation of new political parties and taken control of all German state governments. In October,

Hitler announced that Germany would be leaving the League of Nations.

The following year, 1934, Hitler began sending any remaining political opponents to the hastily built 'wild camps', forerunners of the more permanent concentration camps that were to follow later. But he also perceived enemies in his own camp and, on the weekend of 29 and 30 June, launched the so-called 'Night of the Long Knives' against the leadership of the SA. By now a force of some four million men, its leader Ernst Röhm and others were potentially dangerous rivals, and Hitler had been alerted to this by the suspicions of leading officers in the army. Squads of SS men murdered up to 400 people that weekend, including Röhm and many others who had no association with the SA.

On 1 August, the cabinet enacted a law abolishing the office of president and combining its powers with those of the chancellor. Thus, Hitler became head of state as well as the head of government, giving him full control of the legislative and executive branches of government. The following day, Paul von Hindenburg died and Hitler anointed himself as the supreme leader (Führer) of Germany. Following the announcement, the army swore an oath of personal loyalty to him. This marked the start of the Third Reich.

DICTATORSHIP BEGINS

Even though Hitler did not come to power with a huge democratic majority, within a year he had assumed complete power in Germany. He then used his skills as an orator to persuade the German people that he was there to restore their country to its former glory. 'After 15 years of despair, a great people is back on its feet', he declared shortly after his election.

With the country in ruins, mass unemployment, starvation and continuing political upheaval, Hitler began to address the economic problems and find jobs for the six million unemployed. He used huge rallies to share his vision of the new Germany, peopled by the Aryan master race who would live well and re-establish the traditional values and culture that had been lost. He spoke of his pride in the past and his dreams for the future. It was a message of hope to many of those who had suffered the horrors of war and revolution that they had experienced. All the people were asked to do was accept the harsh measures needed to deal with those who had caused the country's problems – politicians, the Allies, communists, bankers, speculators and Jews – restore order and do what they were told. In reality, Hitler's 'vision' was somewhat different. For him, the posters and slogans of the Nazi propaganda machine had been a means to an end . . . obtaining power. Now he had done that, he had a darker purpose in mind.

In the early years of the Nazi regime, despite the loss of a few personal freedoms, life in Germany was relatively normal. Unemployment came down and the country was gradually freeing itself from the disappointments of the last few years. Tourists flocked to the 'new' Germany and tended to be impressed; the country even hosted the Olympic Games in 1936 to much international acclaim. People did, however, harbour a few doubts: the threat of the Gestapo was a worry, as was the existence of the concentration camps which were regularly written about, particularly in the foreign press. The treatment of the Jews, too, particularly when enshrined in the Nuremberg Laws of September 1935, was disturbing to many. However, as Hitler had intended, with the economy picking up and life gradually returning to normal, most Germans either supported

Nazi policies or at least tolerated them in the belief that they were good for the country.

CULTURE AND PROPAGANDA

The Nazis were keen to infiltrate and control all areas of life in Germany, and that included culture and the arts. The Weimar Republic and Berlin in particular had seen a flourishing of German painting, much of it abstract, and of literature, architecture, music, dance, drama, film, the sciences and philosophy. The Nazis found much of this decadent, subversive and immoral. In 1933, they set up the Reich Chamber of Culture, which was under the control of Goebbels and the Propaganda Ministry, to police the artistic output of Nazi Germany and ensure that it supported their ideals. The tensions of this era are covered dramatically in Bob Fosse's 1972 film *Cabaret*.

In general, the Nazis' attitudes towards culture were anti-intellectual. They were only interested in simple and traditional aspects of German culture – glorifying peasant life, family, heroism on the battlefield and Aryan racial purity – rejecting innovation as subversive. In literature, which they saw as a primary source of education, they blacklisted authors they did not approve of, such as Marxist playwright Bertolt Brecht and Nobel Prize-winning author Thomas Mann, and encouraged mass book burnings across the country. In 1936, they carried out a review of all fine art in German museums and galleries. As a result, some 16,000 paintings were removed from the walls and confiscated. Many of these were later sold on the international art market as a source of foreign currency. Artists approved of by the party had to apply for a licence to produce and sell their work.

During the years before the war, German cinemas and theatres were forced to feature works of National Socialist directors and producers. However, the greatest innovations came in the film work of Leni Riefenstahl. Though mostly producing works of Nazi propaganda, such as *Triumph of the Will* featuring the 1934 Nuremberg Rally, and *Olympia*, which covered the 1936 Games in Berlin, Riefenstahl became famous for her use of innovative techniques and her brilliant directing. Her work was so striking and powerful that she has forever been associated with National Socialism despite being shocked by the violence she witnessed while filming in Poland in the first months of the war, which caused her to withdraw support for the regime.

In architecture, Albert Speer, who was destined to become a member of Hitler's inner circle, designed and built the new Reich Chancellery and the Nazi Party rally grounds in Nuremberg. These were typical buildings of the National Socialist movement, monumental and brutalist in an attempt to convey the 'enduring grandeur' of the movement. Similar grandeur was required of favoured musicians and composers. Works by giants of the German musical canon such as Bach, Beethoven, Bruckner and Richard Wagner, in particular, were promoted, while works by non-Aryans such as Mendelssohn and Mahler, plus jazz and swing music, were repressed at first and then banned altogether.

For historian Karl Bracher, the success of Nazi ideology can only really be understood through its use of the media and culture. He points to their use of modern techniques of opinion-formation to create a 'truly religio-psychological phenomenon' with propaganda as its 'gospel', making it so powerful. Of course, fear was added to the mix but, in reality, that would only give compliance, whereas what the Nazis mainly achieved was internal belief. An even more modern interpretation is that Nazism functioned as a brand.

HITLER'S REAL VISION

With the success of the Olympics and the approbation of visiting foreign leaders, including Lloyd George, who praised him as a 'great man' following a meeting the same year, Hitler's real vision was taking shape. From the perspective of the 21st century, it seems ridiculous to say it, but what he was after was . . . world domination. His aims, hidden in plain sight in *Mein Kampf*, were for a greater Germany populated by 'racially pure' Aryans who would pledge allegiance to the state and to him as their leader. His plan was that Germany would 'move through the world as a peace-loving angel, but one armed with iron and steel'. There could be no opposition; anyone who opposed the regime would be terrorized. Germany would rearm and expand eastwards, waging war on the USSR to destroy communism and build an empire.

Before turning his attention to his foreign policy, there was much still to be done at home. In order to establish their totalitarian state, the Nazis used a number of powerful organizations to rule the German people. At local level, Nazis took control of the police, magistrates, judges and the courts, and were therefore able to punish their opponents and ignore crimes committed by their own agents. Alongside this was the Gestapo, the secret state police, established by Hermann Göring in 1933 and a job taken over the following year by Heinrich Himmler. Much feared by German citizens, the Gestapo used ruthless methods to become a vital part of Nazi repression. Despite being a small organization, it acted as the Nazi police force though it did not answer to any judicial or legal body. It was free to arrest people and send them to concentration camps without trial or even explanation.

Much bigger and more powerful was the SS, also under Himmler, which had been formed in 1925 and was made up of fanatics with particular loyalty to Hitler. Initially providing him with personal protection, the SS grew into a powerful and feared force. At its peak, the SS had a million members across its three divisions: the SD, its internal security service; the Death's Head units, which ran the concentration camps; and the Waffen-SS, armoured regiments that served alongside the regular army (the Wehrmacht).

The ultimate weapon of the Nazi police state, however, was the threat of the concentration camps. The first were set up in disused factories and warehouses soon after Hitler took power, to hold political opponents of the new regime. Purpose-built camps followed and became filled with the regime's enemies: Jews, communists, socialists and others who were sentenced to hard labour. Badly fed, treated with inhumane cruelty and often death, some 1.3 million German citizens were sent to these camps in the first five or six years of their existence.

IN THE GRIP

The Nazis continued to consolidate their power through a combination of propaganda and fear: propaganda, whether through newspapers, radio, films and posters, was controlled by the Party and told people what to think; and fear, stirred up by the violence people saw on the streets or the treatment of the Jews, made sure they did not criticize the regime.

Tests of the support of the German people for Hitler's regime then came thick and fast. In reality, the turnaround in

Germany's economic prospects was built on the manufacture of armaments in preparation for war. This had been in operation since 1934 in complete contravention of the rules set down at Versailles. In 1936, Hitler broke another of the treaty's rules when he sent German troops to reoccupy the demilitarized zone of the Rhineland on Germany's south-west border with France. No one stopped them.

A similar turning point, though much more shocking, occurred in the first week of November 1938. On 7 November, a young Jew, Herschel Grynszpan, killed a German diplomat, Ernst vom Rath, in Paris in revenge for his father's deportation to Poland. Two nights later, the Nazis meted out violent revenge throughout Germany in an anti-Semitic frenzy. Thousands of Jewish homes, schools, businesses, hospitals, synagogues and cemeteries were torched or vandalized. At least a hundred Jews were murdered that night, others were injured and there were numerous rapes. Police officers and firefighters were ordered not to intervene unless there was a threat to Aryan interests. In addition, more than 30,000 Jewish men were arrested and sent to the newly built concentration camps at Buchenwald and Sachsenhausen.

On the morning of 10 November, the streets of Jewish communities were covered in broken glass, giving rise to the name *Kristallnacht*. Göring announced that the German-Jewish community was to blame for the violence, and imposed a collective fine of a billion marks, effectively removing them from the economy. There was outrage at the news of this atrocity throughout the world, but no one spoke up in Germany.

Alarm bells were already ringing in other parts of Europe and in the US. The annexation of Austria had begun on 12 March 1938, the Sudetenland – a resource-rich, German-speaking part of Czechoslovakia – followed in October. By the end of the year, the whole of the country was in Nazi hands. War was inevitable.

WORLD CONFLICT

World War II officially started on 1 September 1939, when Britain and France declared war following the German invasion of Poland. Other countries soon succumbed to the German dogs of war: Denmark, Norway, the Netherlands and Belgium all fell by May 1940. The German war machine was in full operation, and successes on the battlefield meant happy, healthy people at home. Food was plentiful; morale was high.

It is a supreme irony that the seeds of Hitler's eventual defeat were sown the moment he attempted to reach out for his ultimate goal, the invasion of the Soviet Union and the destruction of the communist threat. The German offensive, launched in June 1941, had been planned as a war of annihilation and was notable for its brutality, particularly against Jews, Gypsies and Slavs. The largest military operation of the conflict, Operation Barbarossa as it was known, involved more than three million troops. Within a year German forces were within reach of Moscow. As part of the campaign, mobile death squads called *Einsatzgruppen* were organized to begin the mass murder of Soviet Jews. Comprised of SS troops operating behind the advancing front lines, these units were said to have killed over a million civilians during the German advance through Soviet-occupied Poland, the Baltic states, Ukraine and Russia itself – actions now regarded as the beginning of Hitler's Final Solution policy to rid Europe of the Jewish race. The scorched earth policy adopted by the Wehrmacht was not subject to the normal rules of war, and resulted in the deaths of millions of Soviet civilians and prisoners of war.

In September 1942, German troops reached the outskirts of Stalingrad, marking the most easterly point of their domination. In November, Soviet forces launched a counter-offensive, trapping and destroying an entire German army. The *Blitzkrieg* ('lightning war') was over and the Germans were in catastrophic retreat. Because of the astonishing levels of cruelty that the Germans showed during their advance, the Red Army showed no mercy to the retreating soldiers and the atrocities continued. During the course of the three-year campaign on the Eastern Front, 5.5 million German soldiers and 1.5 million civilians lost their lives. Very few German families were untouched by these losses.

Whether it was the failure of the Luftwaffe to win the Battle of Britain in 1940, the defeat of the Wehrmacht at Stalingrad in 1942–43 or the Normandy Landings in June 1944 that marked the turning point of the war, Germany remained firmly in the grip of Hitler and the Nazi regime. Despite these defeats, the propaganda effort remained powerful. Hitler's personal reputation remained intact, with many of his more fanatical followers still in thrall to him. The Nazification of Germany had sunk deep roots – even deeper that those sown by the fear of violence. After the war, Albert Speer, by then Hitler's minister of armaments and war production, explained the Nazis' hold over the German people, claiming, 'that what distinguished the Third Reich from all previous dictatorships was its use of all the means of communication to sustain itself and to deprive its objects of the power of independent thought'. Nazi influence was everywhere, not just via the Party but also in the layers of officialdom and state bureaucracy. They controlled all areas of life, leaving no personal free space for the ordinary citizen.

THE EXISTENCE OF RESISTANCE

In the autumn of 1944, the German armies were in retreat on both the Eastern and Western Fronts. News brought back by soldiers returning from the fighting was not good. Allied bombing raids were increasing in number and effectiveness. An all-out air assault, which had begun in 1942, targeted both civilian and industrial sites to terrorize the population and to cripple industry. The impact on Germany's war economy was significant as iron and steel production went into decline. With more workers and power needed for the armaments factories, there was less for the civilian population. Food became scarce. The natural result of this was that an increasing number of German citizens began to doubt victory, with an increasing number simply wanting the war to end.

Up to this point, what criticism there was of the Nazi regime had not been aimed at Hitler. According to historian Ian Kershaw, the 'Hitler Myth' that saw him as defender of Germany and liberator of the Fatherland from the shackles of the Treaty of Versailles had held. On 20 July 1944, however, his grip loosened when he was injured after a bomb, placed under his table at a military briefing in East Prussia, exploded. This was part of a plot led by army officer Claus von Stauffenberg to assassinate Hitler and remove the Nazis from power. Although the attempted coup failed, Hitler survived and Stauffenberg and some of his fellow conspirators were executed, the incident proved the existence of resistance to the Nazis inside the party. For many, faith in the Nazi regime and the omnipotence of its leader was shaken.

During the autumn of 1944, bad news continued to arrive from the front line: defeats on the battlefield, lack of men, lack of munitions. At home, the night-time bombing was relentless;

a shortage of gas, lack of fuel and the further disruption of transport all continued to make civilian life depressing, as did the growing prospect of industrial and economic collapse. At a higher level in the Nazi hierarchy, however, faith in Hitler still seemed to hold strong. Whether this faith was real or not is not clear. What is clear is that by this time those in important Party positions had realized that if he went down, then so did they. Hitler's response to the worsening news was to call for all-out war, subordinating all civilian resources and infrastructure to the needs of the military and the war effort, at the same time freeing up the military to use any means necessary to achieve victory.

In September, Hitler decided to forgo defence on the Western Front and turn it into attack. In December, German forces began an offensive, aiming to drive a wedge between British and US forces in the Ardennes, a border region between Belgium and north-eastern France. The Germans launched a surprise attack, using tanks and troops and taking advantage of bad weather, which prevented the use of Allied air support for US troops stationed there. However, they encountered fierce defence which delayed the advance, and improving weather conditions permitted air attacks on German forces and their supply lines. By the middle of January, what became known as the Battle of the Bulge was over and the Germans were in full retreat.

IN PLAIN SIGHT

There was little to celebrate in Germany during New Year 1944–45. It was freezing cold, conditions made worse with no gas, no electricity and little water or food. City streets were flooded with refugees. Hopes, stoked by propaganda promising the imminent arrival of new superweapons, V-2 flying bombs and sophisticated U-boats, were fading. In January, it was announced that Russia had mounted an offensive and its troops were advancing westwards towards Germany. The progress of the Red Army was relentless; by 19 January they had taken Krakow in Poland. Fear of their advance, already stoked by propaganda portraits of the barbaric Bolsheviks, grew further with stories of the astonishing and hideous violence of the advancing forces reported by soldiers returning from the Front. There were regular reports of atrocities committed using maximum brutality, villages burned down, innocent civilians summarily executed and women and girls raped – it is thought that at least 100,000 people died in this manner as Soviet soldiers took revenge for the 'no mercy' tactics shown by the Germans during their invasion. On 27 January, Russian forces arrived at Auschwitz. Although it was not the first concentration camp to be liberated, the size and scale of the operation discovered by the Red Army soldiers that day has ensured that Auschwitz-Birkenau remains a potent symbol of the horrors of the Holocaust (see Chapter 3).

As the Russians crossed the German border from Poland, retreating Wehrmacht soldiers were joined by civilians fearful of the advancing Bolsheviks. For some, this fear galvanized them to fight on out of dread at what might happen to them at the hands of brutal invaders, but for many, Hitler's leadership had lost its shine. By this time, state bureaucracy had completely broken down, evacuation plans were abandoned and there was chaos in the streets of East Prussian towns, which made matters much worse. Finally, the pendulum had begun to swing against the Nazi Party.

As German forces returned home, the country shrank in the face of advancing Allied forces in the west and Soviet forces in the east. Leaders of the Nazi regime, now facing the probability of defeat, meted out increasing violence on those finally turning against them. Repression practised in the east now turned first on the legions of foreign workers, then prisoners of war and then on the German people themselves. During January and February, the shrinking German state was witness to what historian Ian Kershaw described as an 'orgy of killing'; there were summary executions by shooting or hanging for criticism of the regime, defeatism and desertion from the army – it is

And the angels wept... The skeletal remains of the once-beautiful city of Dresden after repeated Allied bombing raids, 1944.

thought that more than 20,000 German soldiers were executed during the last year of the war. Disputes between retreating soldiers and Nazi Party members increased in the confusion.

The situation worsened between 13 and 15 February, when the Allied bombing campaign targeted the city of Dresden using 800 bombers and 2,700 tons of explosives. As a major centre of the road and rail network, the city's destruction was intended to disrupt communication routes, cause chaos for the German authorities and hasten the end of the war. Since the demise of the Luftwaffe and the shambles of what remained of anti-aircraft defences, there was little in the way of protection for the inhabitants. The dropping of so many bombs and incendiary devices caused thousands of small fires, which merged into a firestorm so powerful that its winds sucked oxygen, fuel, broken structures and people into its flames. The city was razed to the ground, and it is estimated that some 25,000 people were killed. The bombing succeeded in terrorizing German civilians both locally and nationwide. The end of the war was in plain sight.

CHAPTER 2

THE DISINTEGRATION OF COMMAND

On 16 January 1945, Hitler took up residence in a converted air raid shelter near the Reich Chancellery in Berlin. The 3,000 square foot reinforced bunker complex, known as the Führerbunker, was his home for the last hundred days of his life. As the centre of the Nazi regime from that day, it was from here that Hitler ran the last months of the war. As well as the Führer and his girlfriend Eva Braun, the bunker's residents included officers and support staff. Visitors, most likely to be political and military leaders, came and went. With defeat becoming increasingly inevitable and the prospect of death ever more likely, the atmosphere in the rooms 50 feet below the gardens of the Chancellery was intensely claustrophobic.

Despite the deteriorating situation, Hitler maintained his manic optimism, determined to continue his attempt to pursue death or glory. The remaining members of the leadership were not so sure, some considering their own positions and those of their country after the war, though they kept these thoughts to themselves.

As tensions increased, some began to argue among themselves, looking for ways out; Heinrich Himmler, Joachim von Ribbentrop and Göring all considered negotiating with the Allies. Only Goebbels remained steadfast in his support. With differing intentions among the regime leadership, Hitler's orders were often not carried out, and some were not even delivered – his crown was slipping. Matters came to a head in March. Throughout his life, Adolf Hitler had never been able to admit mistakes or accept responsibility for any failure. His morale was finally in decline, and as the thousand-year Reich he founded teetered on the brink of collapse, he blamed it on the weakness of the German people and a military organization riddled with timid, disloyal and incompetent officers. If only they had really listened to him and let themselves be inspired. If only they had possessed the same will and determination as he possessed, everything would have turned out differently.

With so little faith in the German people and the Allies now on German soil, Hitler ordered the Wehrmacht to destroy the country's transport infrastructure, rendering factories, bridges, electricity supplies and water installations useless rather than have them fall into enemy hands. Armaments minister Albert Speer, who visited the bunker in March to speak directly to Hitler, was clear in his belief that Germany's infrastructure and its people should be protected from destruction. Hitler was enraged, and on 19 March issued his 'Nero decree' ordering the evacuation of civilians and the complete destruction of everything in areas threatened by Allied forces.

By April, all that was left of Germany was a narrow strip of land from Norway in the north to northern Italy in the south, with the Allies closing in on Berlin. In the east, 15 April saw the beginning of the Soviet push for the capital, while in the west Nuremberg fell to US forces on 20 April and other cities began to surrender without resistance. The atmosphere in the bunker and the city at large became increasingly hysterical and fatalistic. Although many of those present in the bunker with the Führer had no intention of dying with him and were making plans to get away, they kept silent about their intentions.

Hitler's influence on the Wehrmacht and the Waffen-SS, however, continued to hold sway, and they put up fierce resistance against both the invaders and those Germans who were no longer prepared to fight. No soldier wanted Germany to be defeated, least of all by the Bolsheviks in the east where the propaganda war had been so effective. Hitler's most loyal generals, including Model, Schörner, Schultz, Kesselring, Jodl, Keitel and Dönitz, were prepared to fight to the end.

NOTHING LEFT TO LIVE FOR

The end came in the last two weeks of April. Nazi Party functionaries began to abandon their posts, many fleeing for their lives. In the increasingly violent streets, Nazis had become openly unpopular and in some towns the Party was disbanded. The situation grew more and more chaotic, with retreating German soldiers abandoning their uniforms and mingling with evacuated civilians and refugees from Austria and Hungary fleeing from the advancing forces. Uncontrolled violence during these days led to the deaths of hundreds of civilians.

Hitler had now been joined in the bunker by Joseph Goebbels, his wife Magda and their six children, along with deputy Führer Martin Bormann, a doctor, two secretaries and Hitler's vegetarian cook. Matters among the elite of the Nazi Party leadership had come to a head. On 23 April, Hitler dismissed Göring from his post, furious that his appointed successor was actually attempting to take over as leader. Himmler suffered a similar fate when it was discovered that he had colluded with a Swedish diplomat and had been promised his freedom in return for releasing 30,000 people from the concentration camps.

By 25 April, Berlin's suburbs had fallen and the Red Army was closing in on the centre of the city. Fierce fighting continued, with members of the Hitler Youth and the old men of the *Volkssturm* obeying the Führer's orders to fight to the last man. Sometime after midnight on 29 April, Hitler and Eva Braun made their marriage vows in front of eight guests, including Goebbels and Bormann. They were then toasted with champagne to the accompaniment of the thumps of artillery shells overhead. After the ceremony, Hitler handed out small glass capsules filled with cyanide to everyone around him and declared his intention to remain where he was and die rather than be captured by the enemy. Around 3:30 on the afternoon of 30 April, with the bunker shuddering under the ceaseless barrage of Soviet artillery, after speaking quietly to Bormann, Goebbels and others, Adolf Hitler and his wife Eva went into his room. Hitler watched as Eva bit down on a cyanide capsule before putting a revolver in his mouth and pulling the trigger. Rochus Misch, a member of the SS and of Hitler's guard, recalled, 'Everyone was waiting for the shot, we were expecting it... Then came the shot. Heinz Linge [Hitler's valet] took me to one side and we went in. I saw Hitler slumped by the table. I didn't see any blood on his head. I saw Eva with her knees drawn up lying next to him on the sofa...' With great difficulty, soldiers dragged Hitler's body up to the Chancellery garden above and put it in a shallow shell hole. Martin Bormann followed with Eva's corpse. The bodies were doused in gasoline and set on fire.

Earlier in the year, Magda Goebbels had written a letter to her son by another marriage, saying, 'The world that comes after the Führer and National Socialism is no longer worth living in...' The day after Hitler's death, Magda arranged for her six children to have injections of morphine before being administered with lethal doses of cyanide. When the deed was done, she and Joseph went up to the garden and took cyanide together. His adjutant then shot them, to make sure, after which they too were doused in gasoline and burned.

A few made it out of the bunker, including Martin Bormann. His dead body was found nearby on 2 May, but it had to wait until 1973 before it was confirmed as Bormann's (reaffirmed in 1998 by a DNA test). A witness claimed that Bormann and a colleague had come across Soviet troops as they made their escape and swallowed cyanide capsules to avoid capture.

THE FIGHTING STOPS

The news of Hitler's death was announced by his successor, Grand-Admiral Karl Dönitz, on German radio on 1 May. He said, 'It is reported from Der Führer's headquarters that our Führer Adolf Hitler, fighting to the last breath against Bolshevism, fell for Germany this afternoon in his operational headquarters in the Reich Chancellery.' The fighting stopped on 9 May 1945, leaving Germany in ruins. With the Party leaders dead, fear among its functionaries and ordinary members was palpable. Having shed their uniforms, torn down their portraits of the Führer and done as much as possible to play down their affiliations with the Party, they had few choices: stay where they were and face arrest and execution; hide within Germany, try to flee overseas or suicide, an example plainly set by their former leaders. Many Germans followed suit as an epidemic of suicides

An American soldier plays the part of Adolf Hitler on the balcony of the Reich Chancellery in Berlin, where the Nazi leader once proclaimed his 1,000-year empire, 1945. A British and Russian soldier stand on either side of him.

spread across the country. Suicide had been a feature of Nazism since the Party's formation, among German Jews at the outbreak of the war and the start of deportations, and among the officers involved in the attempt to assassinate Hitler in July 1944. As the regime began to crumble in the last months of the war, the idea of suicide served as a sign of heroic self-sacrifice, a manly act to show others that without Hitler and National Socialism life was not worth living. It was seen as a heroic death and was the route chosen by politicians, SS leaders, members of the police force, army and Luftwaffe generals and admirals. Göring and Himmler took the same route out while in Allied captivity.

But there were other reasons for this epidemic of self-immolation, particularly for those in the east whose fears of the advancing Red Army had been stirred up to fever pitch by anti-Bolshevik propaganda. Goebbels, in charge of Nazi propaganda, encouraged German citizens to kill themselves rather than fall into Russian captivity. Historian Florian Huber revealed that more than 1,000 of Demmin's 15,000 residents killed themselves as the Soviet soldiers approached the north German town. Usually they took poison, and that was sometimes provided by the local authorities; others hanged, shot or drowned themselves in the region's many rivers and lakes. There were suicides, too, in cities, towns and villages on the Western Front; these included senior officials of the Nazi Party, rank and file members and ordinary citizens who fervently believed in Nazi ideology and feared for the future under occupation. In Berlin itself, some 10,000 people are believed to have killed themselves in the first four months of 1945.

ONE OF THE FIRST

Until the first weeks of 1945, the Nazi regime, although always chaotic, seemed to hold together. With the failure of the Ardennes offensive, almost all Germans, apart from Hitler, believed that the war was most likely to be lost. While trying to remain positive in public, in private many of the regime's leaders were having doubts about their own personal futures.

Helene or 'Helli' Bouhler was a tall woman who always dressed in a simple, elegant way and wore her hair in the traditional *Hausfrau* style that had been fashionable and almost compulsory in Hitler's Germany since 1933. On 19 May 1945, she was standing at one of the upper windows of the castellated Schloss Fischorn in western Austria. She had been arrested there by American troops nine days earlier. She was now looking down towards the cold Alpine waters of the Zeller See a mile or so away to the north. Somewhere near the lake in the forests down below was the military detention camp where her husband Philipp had been taken into custody.

As she and her husband had made their way as fugitives from Berlin to Bavaria and then Austria, Helene had already imagined her future in the defeated and shattered remains of the Reich. For more than a decade, she had led a gilded life as one of the brightest and prettiest stars at Hitler's court. She had often been photographed in his company. She was an intimate friend of many of the leading figures among the social elite of Nazi Germany, particularly Hermann and Emmy Göring. Although little known outside Hitler's inner circle, her husband had long been one of the most important cogs in the Nazi Party machine and was guilty of masterminding some of the regime's worst crimes. As a committed member of the 'master race', Helene could expect little compassion from the victorious

Allies. There was very little for her to look forward to in the ruined Germany that they would control. Everything she had believed in and had loved was lost. Prominent supporters of the vanquished Nazi regime such as she would be social pariahs. She expected lengthy interrogation followed by the misery of imprisonment. At some point that day, she was informed that Philipp had committed suicide and she made her own decision. Opening the window wide, she flung herself downwards on to the gravel courtyard of the castle four floors below. Once the brief paperwork recording her death was complete and her one remaining ring detached from her finger, her body was loaded up on to a truck and taken to be dumped in one of the mass graves at Dachau.

If his wife's suicide was influenced by her fears for the future, Philipp Bouhler's decision to kill himself was based on his correct understanding that his long years of outstanding service to National Socialism marked him out in Allied eyes as a war criminal of the first rank. He had been one of the very first of Hitler's followers, an early contributor to the Nazi newspaper the *Völkischer Beobachter* ('People's Observer') and was said to hold party membership card number 12. Later photographs showed him proudly wearing the Golden Badge that was awarded to those who had belonged to the NSDAP since its earliest days. When Hitler emerged from Landsberg Prison in 1925 and began to rebuild his movement, one of his first acts was to make Bouhler the national manager of the Nazi Party organization, a complex administrative job at which he excelled. After taking complete control of Germany as Führer in 1934, Hitler kept the efficient and discreet Bouhler close to his side as chief of his own chancellery, where he dealt with Hitler's private papers and most secret correspondence. Bouhler was also trusted to chair the important Nazi board that screened all publications in the Third Reich and censored anything that contravened party guidelines.

REMOVING THE 'USELESS MOUTHS'

In late 1939, a new set of duties were added to Bouhler's remit, which placed him right at the heart of the Nazi programme of mass murder. Working with Hitler's physician Karl Brandt, he was made responsible for planning and implementing a secret programme – given the codename Aktion T4 after its head office address in Tiergartenstrasse in Berlin. Prompted by the Nazi obsession with racial purity and hygiene, Aktion T4 involved the systematic euthanasia or forced killing of 'useless mouths', such as hospital and asylum inmates with incurable conditions who were, in Hitler's view, an unnecessary drain on the resources of the Reich. Although Aktion T4 officially ended in 1941, the state murder of men, women and children with physical and mental disabilities by injection, gassing and in some cases by shooting continued until 1945. Recent research suggests that the total number of deaths in the Reich and in occupied eastern Europe brought about by Aktion T4 and later related euthanasia programmes was well over 300,000. Thanks in large part to Bouhler's meticulous organizational skills, the programme was, in Nazi terms, an outstanding success. In the view of National Socialist thinkers, Aktion T4 was a major step towards purifying the bloodstock of the German people by eliminating the insane and the disabled. Large numbers of valuable hospital beds had also been freed up for wartime use by the Wehrmacht and SS. Crucially, many useful lessons had been learned as to how best to collect, assess, liquidate and dispose of large numbers of unwanted people. Bouhler's conscientious work and his subsequent detailed reports laid the foundations for the efficient destruction of European Jewry in the coming Holocaust.

Philipp and Helene Bouhler were typical of a tranche of leading Nazis who followed Hitler's example and chose suicide as their method of evading Allied justice. Given the chaotic conditions that prevailed throughout Europe in the last months of war and the first days of 'peace', the exact number of Nazi suicides defies accurate measurement. However, in the eight months from April to December 1945, over a hundred important members of the Nazi machine, party functionaries, key figures in the SS, participants in the extermination programmes plus a coterie of Nazi ideologues and theorists, killed themselves rather than risk ending their days in an Allied prison or on an Allied scaffold. Many of these suicides were senior officers in the German armed forces who felt under particular pressure to end it all quickly.

THE 'FÜHRER'S FIREMAN'

On 4 April 1945, two vast Allied armies met up at Lippstadt just over 80 miles east of the Rhine. Their successful pincer thrust had encircled and trapped the German forces that defended the valley of the river Ruhr, the industrial heartland of the Reich. Omar Bradley and Bernard Montgomery, the Allied generals charged with capturing the Ruhr, enjoyed an overwhelming advantage in terms of numbers on the ground and air superiority. Against them was a much smaller, depleted force, running low on munitions and machines. Many of the German defenders that were now surrounded by the Allies were merely *Volkssturm*, members of a national militia made up of older civilian militiamen armed with obsolete hunting rifles and pistols, their numbers bolstered by inexperienced boys of the Hitler Youth. Nevertheless, their morale was surprisingly high. They were fighting on home ground that most of them knew well. The Führer had promised that a newly formed army was already on its way to the Ruhr Pocket, bearing the long-awaited wonder-weapons that would soon have the Allies running backwards to the Atlantic. He called on the men of Fortress Ruhr to defend Germany's western lands with determination. And he reminded them that they were being led by his most successful field commander, the grim Prussian Field Marshal Walter Model.

Most German generals had seemed to be invincible in the victorious early months of the war, when the enemy was merely an isolated Poland fighting on two fronts or the unprepared and unsure democracies in Scandinavia, Belgium and the Netherlands. Fighting Stalinist Russia had turned out to be a much more difficult proposition, and the slugfest on the Eastern Front had exposed the limitations of many German commanders. As the war developed, the austere Model emerged as a tough and unyielding leader when the Wehrmacht was already on the back foot after Stalingrad. Model was a masterful defensive tactician, and his ability to shore things up and damp down the flames in a crisis, such as the collapse of Army Group Centre in Belorussia in summer 1944 or the unexpected appearance of an airborne paratroop army near Arnhem that autumn, had earned him the nickname the 'Führer's fireman'.

By this late stage in the war, however, even Model could do little to defend the Ruhr Pocket given the meagre resources at his disposal. Many of his infantrymen were running out of ammunition; the few remaining active Panzer tanks had little fuel. Crucially, the help promised by Hitler never arrived. US

Army loudspeakers near the front lines were soon encouraging Model's dispirited men to lay down their arms, and on 14 April they began to respond in ever larger numbers. The following day his supporting officers began to disappear or surrender. The pressures on Model over the next few days were typical of those facing many senior Wehrmacht commanders in the spring of 1945. An American communiqué on 15 April offered him the chance to save German lives and cities by ordering his troops to stand down at once. The Allied message hinted at clemency, and a number of his senior officers urged him at least to speak to the enemy. Model stalled but used the time he gained to save as many of his men as possible, discharging the boys and the elderly men from their military duties and encouraging them to make their way home in civilian clothing. On 17 April, he ordered the troops in his remaining functioning units to break out from the Ruhr and seek their own salvation, thereby disobeying Hitler's explicit command to resist to the very end. In fact, most of Model's troops had already given themselves up to the Allies and were now being gathered together in vast makeshift prison camps in the rolling meadows of the Ruhr.

THE DEATH OF A SOLDIER

Later that day, Model sat with his chief of staff and discussed his personal position. Like all men of the Wehrmacht, he had sworn an oath of loyalty to the Führer. Even now, especially with the war clearly lost, he had no wish to dishonour his oath despite the fact that Hitler had broken his promise to provide support. Moreover, Model was very aware that in the past he had often publicly scorned the defeated General Paulus for surrendering at Stalingrad, thus becoming the first German Field Marshal in history to be captured alive. Model had no wish to be remembered as a second cowardly failure. He was also aware that the Soviets almost certainly planned to indict him for war crimes committed in the central sector of the Russian Front in 1942 and 1943, where he had followed a rigorous scorched earth policy that involved poisoning civilian water supplies, burning crops and executing unarmed civilians suspected of partisan activity. There was no guarantee that the Americans would not hand him over to Moscow. In Russia he could expect to be shot or hanged on arrival. Under great pressure, that night he was heard to mutter about the historic fate of defeated generals, 'in ancient times they took poison'. After eluding the Allies for several days, at a brief meeting on 21 April near Duisburg, Field Marshall Model ordered his aides to scatter, before walking into a small wood of Rhineland oaks and putting an end to his troubles with his Walther 6.35mm service pistol.

THE FATE OF THE DEFEATED COMMANDERS

As the German armed forces in the west were ground down by logistics and the logic of war, the highly decorated Panzer commander General Karl Decker also found himself trapped in the Ruhr Pocket. Decker had enjoyed notable success in the fall of France and in the dirty war in the Balkans. On the Russian Front, he had earned a reputation as a quick-thinking and determined commander. In happier times, Hitler had praised him in Napoleonic terms as 'a lucky general'. However, his supply of munitions and good fortune both ran out in the middle weeks of April 1945. When the last of his units finally disintegrated and his men had dispersed or surrendered, he slipped away to his family home near Braunschweig, where he followed Model's example and blew his brains out on 21 April.

General Erich Bärenfänger was a staunch National Socialist who waged war as ferociously as he could until he too ran out of the means to do so. In the final days of the Red Army assault on Berlin, Bärenfänger was in command of what remained of German forces among the rubble of the city's south-eastern suburbs. Only 30 years old, he was the youngest general in the Wehrmacht. He was also almost certainly the last German general to launch a successful attack in World War II, managing to gather together sufficient men and tanks to halt and then push the Russians back from several key positions in the city. Witnesses later remembered seeing him in the last days of April standing upright in the cupola of his Panzer urging his men to advance towards certain, pointless death. Once the rumour of Hitler's suicide that had been spreading through Berlin during the last few days of April was confirmed, Bärenfänger and his family attempted to escape. On the evening of 2 May, protected by a small combat squad, they attempted to break out of the city through the subway network. To their horror, they found the way blocked thanks to the SS who had mined the nearby canal and flooded the tunnels at Oranienburger Strasse earlier in the day. After hiding in the grounds of a ruined distillery in the Prenzlauer district and realizing that their group was entirely surrounded by Soviet troops, he, his young wife and her brother shot themselves.

This self-culling of the German military's upper ranks continued throughout the summer months of 1945 thanks to the fusion of despair in defeat and the fear of vengeful Allied justice. The dread inspired by the thought of Soviet justice was especially strong. General Erpo Baron von Bodenhausen played a major role in defending the trapped Courland Pocket in western Latvia throughout ten bloody months of siege and battle against far superior Russian forces. As soon as the order to surrender to the Soviets had been transmitted to his corps on 9 May, he committed suicide within the hour to avoid capture. Similarly, General Arthur Kobus, a respected professional soldier who had come up through the ranks serving the Kaiser, the Weimar Republic and the Third Reich, did away with himself in Berlin in late May. It had become clear to him just how thoroughly the Russians were going to exact revenge on all those who had served Hitler's regime.

THE GUILT OF SURRENDER

If some commanders contemplated suicide because they had failed in their command, two senior officers carried the added burden of being complicit in the surrender of the entire German military. Admiral Hans-Georg von Friedeburg and General Eberhard Kinzel were both in at the very death of the Third Reich. Von Friedeburg had been commander of the German U-boat fleet since early 1943 and was promoted to C-in-C of the Kriegsmarine, or German navy, when Admiral Dönitz became Reich President following Hitler's suicide. Kinzel served in various senior posts on the General Staff of the Wehrmacht. On 1 May, Dönitz appointed both men to his short-lived government based at Flensburg in the small pocket of northern Germany that had not yet fallen into Allied hands. Two days later, both men were members of the delegation sent to Field Marshal Montgomery's HQ near the town of Lüneburg to negotiate the German surrender in north-western Europe. On 4 May, after consulting with their chief, they both signed the unconditional surrender document, which was the only deal on offer from Montgomery. The following week, von Friedeburg was in Reims and then Berlin to witness the signing of the subsequent full surrender documentation. He remained at his post with Dönitz at Flensburg for another two weeks until the Allies dissolved this final vestige of Nazi government on 23 May and promptly arrested its members. Unable to face captivity, von Friedeburg returned to his barracks and bit on his cyanide capsule. Two days later, Kinzel, who had been acting as a liaison officer with Montgomery's Army Group, learned that he was no longer needed by the Allies. Fearing interrogation, imprisonment and separation from his typist and girlfriend, Kinzel also killed himself. His beloved Erika joined him in death.

FORCED SUICIDES

General Heinrich Burchard had already done away with himself several weeks before Hitler, although he had no real say in the matter. Like many German officers in the last weeks of the war, he was not a victim of Allied justice but of Nazi punishment. Originally an army artillery officer, during the last phase of the war he was on special detachment as general of the Luftwaffe's Flak-Division, charged with protecting Germany's cities from the nightly armada of Allied bombers. It was an unenviable command given the limited hardware and manpower available to him. For the German civilians who huddled and grumbled in their underground bomb shelters throughout the last two years of the war, the increasing impotence of the Luftwaffe and its Flak-Division was a nightly, unarguable sign of impending defeat. By 1945, Burchard knew better than most just how little effective protection his Flak gunners could now provide. He himself only narrowly survived the massive Allied bombardment of a supposedly safe small town in the Harz mountains. He was later heard to voice his despair openly, saying that the war in the air was totally lost and that Hitler should put an end to things.

His remarks quickly made their way back to Hermann Göring, who was looking for scapegoats to deflect public criticism of his leadership and the anger of the Führer. Burchard was arrested and tried by one of the special flying military tribunals that were set up to quell dissent and root out defeatists in the ranks. Found guilty on 11 April, he was marched into a sparse room at Güstrow airbase in Mecklenburg north of Berlin. The room contained a small table, a chair and a loaded pistol.

A LOYAL SUICIDE

Like the German navy, in the chaos of late April 1945 the Luftwaffe also received a new, short-lived leader. Believing that Göring had planned a coup against him and was therefore guilty of treason, on 23 April Hitler ordered him to resign from his high offices. The Führer also agreed to arrangements for his arrest and almost certain execution by the SS. In Göring's place, as C-in-C of the Luftwaffe, he appointed one of his most loyal followers, Robert Ritter von Greim, a pioneer fighter ace in World War I, whose skill and bravery had been rewarded with a knighthood and permission to use the aristocratic title of 'von'. Greim was a dedicated Hitlerite who took part in the 1923 Munich Putsch, which first brought Hitler to the attention of the German nation, and had been instrumental in the reconstruction of Germany's airpower in the 1930s. He remained loyal to the Führer until the very end. On 26 April 1945, as most Germans were flooding westwards and busily destroying all evidence of their connection to the defeated regime, von Greim flew into central Berlin in an attempt to rescue Hitler from the Führerbunker. He and his mistress, the acclaimed aviator and devout Nazi Hanna Reitsch, braved their way through Allied fighter cover and the shelling of German

Robert Ritter von Greim was a German field marshal and World War I flying ace. He was appointed head of the Luftwaffe after Hitler sacked Göring for treason, but by then a lack of planes made the position purely honorary.

anti-aircraft batteries. When von Greim was badly injured in the foot by flak, Reitsch only just managed to take over the cockpit controls in time and landed near the Brandenburg Gate, as close as possible to Hitler's underground sanctuary. The Führer refused their offer to fly him out of the city and on to 'safety' in Bavaria, but he appointed von Greim to Göring's former command as head of the Luftwaffe. In reality, it was merely a gesture to thank von Greim for his loyalty, as very little remained of Germany's former air command: when surrounded by American troops at Kitzbühel in the Alps on 8 May, von Greim joked with his captors, 'I am the head of the German Air Force but I have no air force'. In fact, as Commander of the Luftwaffe, his only task for Hitler was to fly to Plön near the Danish border. There, he was to arrest the SS chief Heinrich Himmler who had also fallen foul of the Führer's paranoia. However, as a reward for his bravery in flying into the encircled Berlin, his beloved Führer had given von Greim something much more valuable than a moribund military title. On 24 May and under American arrest in Salzburg, von Greim believed that he was about to be handed over into the custody of the Soviet Red Army. Thanks to Hitler's parting gift of a cyanide capsule, he was able to evade Russian justice.

ANNIHILATION TO THE LAST MAN

Around midnight on the night of 3–4 August 1942, a British motor torpedo boat slipped into a cove beneath the cliffs of Hog's Back, a rocky outcrop on the south-eastern coast of Sark. It carried a select group of British commandos. Their mission had three objectives: to ascertain the strength and readiness of enemy forces on the small Channel Island; take any useful prisoners; and wherever possible, cause mayhem. In the course of their brief invasion of the island, the men of 12 Commando encountered a small detachment of sleeping German troops. They took five prisoners and tied their hands behind their backs. En route back to the beach, one of the captives started shouting for help and was shot dead. Moments later, three of the others broke away trying to escape. Two were shot and one was stabbed. The Commandos eventually succeeded in taking one prisoner back to Blighty on their MTB.

German propaganda immediately claimed that the dead troops had already surrendered yet had been shot by the British in cold blood, having had their hands shackled in irons. Hitler was incensed and used the incident to issue his notorious Commando Order two weeks later. This declared that all enemy personnel captured while engaged in raiding or sabotage activity were to be annihilated to the last man. These prisoners were to be shown no mercy and given no pardon, even if they were in proper military uniform, unarmed and clearly willing to surrender. The unreliable Wehrmacht was forbidden to detain such personnel within their own POW facilities. Captured commandos were to be handed over to the Nazi security services to ensure their immediate execution without trial.

Hitler's Commando Order introduced to the conflict in the west something of the everyday barbarism of total war on the Eastern Front, where both sides regularly butchered prisoners as a matter of course. It also obliged German military commanders to breach the prevailing international regulations governing the treatment of prisoners as defined in the Hague and Geneva conventions. Obeying this order automatically turned German army officers into war criminals. Many welcomed the order and carried it out willingly. Many others simply carried it out with customary military obedience. Some senior Wehrmacht officers, notably Erwin Rommel, were deeply uncomfortable with being forced to implement an order that so blatantly contravened the accepted rules of war – but few of these critics openly disregarded or flouted Hitler's command. There were far too many watchful SS and Gestapo functionaries around, let alone the fanatical Nazis within the ranks of their own units. Most German commanders simply carried out the order and ensured that they were seen to do so with a sufficient degree of the required enthusiasm.

NORWEGIAN PIRATES

Typical of this last group was Admiral Otto von Schrader, who commanded German naval forces on Norway's west coast. His task was to deter the small-scale raiding by sleek and speedy torpedo boats that so irritated the Führer. *MTB 345* was a small vessel of the Royal Norwegian Navy engaged in attacking German shipping and carrying supplies and information to Resistance agents along the coast. In late July 1943, it was forced to abort its mission and take shelter at the island of Ospa north of Bergen, when it ran out of fuel and was unable to return to its base in Shetland. Von Schrader commanded the flotilla of seven German warships that surrounded and captured *MTB 345* and its six Norwegian and one British crewmen. The hit-and-run activity of Allied MTBs along the coasts of occupied Europe was deemed to be 'piratical' rather than military, and therefore von Schrader was obliged to deal with his captives as prescribed by Hitler's Commando Order.

The captured men were quickly handed over to the security services. They were taken to Bergen, where they were tortured and executed on 30 July. That evening, their bodies were dropped into the cold waters of Krossfjord, west of Spitsbergen.

As if acknowledging their guilt in the war crime that had been committed, the Germans attached explosives to the seven corpses and the evidence of their murder was blasted into pieces at the bottom of the sea. Von Schrader was captured by the Norwegians on 17 July 1945. Knowing that he was complicit in a war atrocity, the admiral committed suicide two days later. His Wehrmacht colleague in the *MTB 345* affair, Colonel-General von Falkenhorst, took a different approach when he faced trial for his crimes in 1946. Like many German commanders brought to justice, in his defence Falkenhorst claimed that he was 'only obeying the orders of his superiors'. He was lucky. Although sentenced to death in 1946, an appeal dragged on long enough for the immediate post-war desire for revenge to begin to recede. Eventually his death sentence was commuted to imprisonment for 20 years. He was home by 1953 thanks to purported ill health.

CHAPTER 3

THE WAR CRIMES TRIALS

THE EARLIEST condemnation of Nazi atrocities was made in a joint statement by the exiled Czech and Polish governments in London in November 1940. Keen to help their fellow countrymen by reducing the chances of further atrocities, they lobbied British prime minister Winston Churchill to take action. Churchill raised the idea of establishing a United Nations commission on atrocities during a visit to the US in June 1942.

Poland had suffered unbelievable acts of brutality since 1939 when, as a result of the Molotov–Ribbentrop non-aggression pact, it was invaded by Germany and Russia. The Germans immediately began a campaign of indiscriminate killings, with an estimated 200 people put to death each day during September, including captured soldiers and civilians. These so-called 'pacification' raids on towns and villages were intended to subdue the local population. Picked at random, a few hundred locals were marched to the place of execution, forced to undress and lie face down in pits that had already been dug. They were then shot and their corpses covered with a layer of quick-lime. A second batch of victims was then ordered to lie down on top of the bodies and, after they were killed, another layer of quick-lime was thrown on top. This procedure was repeated until the pit was full. The bodies were then trampled down until the surface was level enough for trees or grass to be planted. Executions such as this were carried out daily by the Nazi death squads as they marched victoriously through Poland, and later the Soviet Union. In the village of Szalas in south-central Poland, for example, male inhabitants over the age of 15, some 300 in all, were rounded up and many were machine-gunned to death; the others were locked in the local school which was then set on fire. To ensure that his orders were carried out, Hitler announced that: 'No German soldier could be brought to trial for any act committed against Polish or Russian citizens.'

The German advance included the burning and looting of over 500 towns and villages. By the end of the year, over 50,000 Poles, many of them Jewish, had been murdered in occupied territory. There was terror from the air, too, as the Luftwaffe targeted over 150 cities, many with no military installations at all. Having dropped their payloads, the German planes joined in the mass killings by strafing people fleeing along the surrounding roads.

Soviet Forces also committed atrocities. The worst was the Katyn massacre in April and May 1940, when the NKVD secret police murdered some 22,000 Polish nationals in a series of mass executions carried out in Katyn Forest near Smolensk. Stalin's plan was to destroy Poland and wipe it from the map through ethnic cleansing. In 1940 and 1941, he ordered the deportation of an estimated 1.5 million Poles to forced labour camps in eastern USSR, the Urals and Siberia. Many died on their journeys, few survived the camps, and those who did were later conscripted into the Red Army.

The situation in Czechoslovakia was similar. While the brutality in Poland was stoked by propaganda, there was particular bitterness over the treatment of over three million ethnic Germans in the province of Sudetenland. In September 1938, this area was ceded to Germany as part of the Munich appeasement effort. As a result, Czechoslovakia ceased to exist and was replace by Slovakia, which was populated mainly by Slovak and Czech ethnic groups, *Untermenschen* ('sub-humans') according to Nazi doctrine.

One of the Hitler's key tactics to ensure cooperation with his occupying forces was the practice of shooting hostages, those arrested to guarantee the future good conduct of their community, and reprisal prisoners who had been arrested to punish any show of resistance. These acts were widespread, brutal and deliberately intended to terrorize the local inhabitants. One of the worst incidents was the destruction of the village of Lidice. On 27 May 1942, two Czech patriots ambushed and threw a bomb at a car carrying Reinhard Heydrich, the Reich Protector of Bohemia and Moravia. Described by Hitler as 'the man with the iron heart' and one of the main architects of the Holocaust, Heydrich's tactics in supressing Czech resistance had been particularly brutal. He died eight days later (see pages 87–8, Chapter 4). Hitler was furious, and in revenge ordered the killing of 10,000 Czech citizens selected at random. Intelligence suggested that Lidice, 10 miles from Prague, may have been a hideout for the killers. On 9 June, police surrounded the village and arrested everyone. The following morning, 196 women and 88 young children were driven away in trucks to concentration camps at Auschwitz and Ravensbrück; four of the women were found to be pregnant and were given forced abortions and then sent to the camps. Later that morning, the men and boys were brought out ten at a time, lined up against a barn wall and shot. Some 200 died that day. While the firing squad was busy, the village was burned to the ground. Ploughs and bulldozers were then brought in to leave no trace of the village of Lidice. Of the children taken away, 17 were selected for 'Germanization' in German households; the other 81 were sent to a camp at Chelmno and gassed. In all, the Nazis arrested more than 3,000 people: 1,357 were shot and another 657 died during interrogation by the SS.

In 1942, details of these atrocities and many others supplied by the Polish government were discussed in the British parliament, along with a proposal for the formation of a United Nations War Crimes Commission. Shortly afterwards, the American, British and Soviet governments made a public declaration 'that explicitly condemned Hitler's ongoing extermination of European Jews'. In October 1943, US president Franklin D. Roosevelt, Winston Churchill and the Soviet premier Joseph Stalin, whose forces had now joined the fight against Germany, signed the Moscow Declaration of German Atrocities. It stated that at the time of an armistice, Germans deemed responsible for atrocities, massacres or executions would be returned to the countries in which the crimes had been committed to be judged and punished according to the laws of the nation concerned. In addition, major war criminals, whose crimes could not be assigned to one particular place, would be dealt with by joint decisions between the Allied governments. The UN War Crimes Commission, comprising nationals of the United Nations selected by their own governments, was formally

One of the main architects of the Holocaust, Reinhard Heydrich was famous for his cruelty. He was ambushed near Prague in 1942 by Czech and Slovak soldiers trained by the British. The Czech village of Lidice was destroyed by Nazis in reprisal for his death.

founded in the same month and charged with investigating and recording, in particular, 'organized atrocities' perpetrated by the Nazi regime. Despite limited powers, it proved to be a landmark in the development of international law.

THE LONDON CHARTER

Although discussions between the three major Allied wartime powers – Britain, the US and the Soviet Union – had taken place at the meetings in Tehran in 1942, Yalta and Potsdam in 1945, there were differences of opinion on punishments to be handed out to those responsible for war crimes during the conflict. Roosevelt favoured the Morgenthau plan, suggested by his Jewish Secretary of the Treasury Henry Morgenthau, who argued for the summary execution of top Nazi leaders. Winston Churchill was in broad agreement with this, but objected to Morgenthau's further idea of destroying Germany's industrial capacity and turning it into 'a country primarily agricultural and pastoral in its character'. US Secretary of War, Henry Stimson, argued strongly for trials, an opinion shared by Joseph Stalin, although the trials he had in mind were more like show trials, in which the outcome has already been decided. In the event, Roosevelt changed his mind in favour of the legal approach, though he did not live to see the end of the conflict and was succeeded in April 1945 by Harry Truman.

The various Allied activities in this area culminated in a meeting of the Commission in London. By then, France had joined what were now the so-called four Great Powers who established the International Military Tribunal (IMT), then agreed the legal, substantive and procedural rules for the impending war trials which were published as the London Charter on 8 August. The Charter listed three categories of crime: Crimes against Peace; War Crimes; and Crimes against Humanity. The Charter also restricted its activities to 'punishment of the major war criminals of the European Axis countries', but the list also included several Nazi organizations which it defined as criminal.

The terms of the London Charter were known as the 'Nuremberg Principles' because the trials were to be held in the Bavarian city. It had been chosen, in preference to Luxembourg, Leipzig and Berlin, because it was home to the suitably sized Palace of Justice, which was largely undamaged and had a prison on site. It remains in use as a courtroom today.

THE ARROGANCE AND CRUELTY OF POWER

The Nuremberg Trials were the first to hold government leaders accountable for their actions during wartime, and this was the first time that the horrors of the Holocaust were discussed in public on a major platform. The IMT trial at Nuremberg began on 20 November 1945. Although it was not the first war crimes trial of World War II – Nazis had been tried and executed in Krasnodar in Russia and in the city of Kharkov in Ukraine – it was the most important. Facing judges and prosecutors from the four main Allied countries were the 24 heads of the Nazi regime who had been captured by the Allies, along with their defence lawyers. Although Hitler, Himmler, Goebbels and Robert Ley (a member of Hitler's inner circle, head of the German Labour Front and deeply implicated in the mistreatment of foreign slave labourers who had hanged himself in captivity before the trial) were already dead, the defendants included Hermann Göring, Rudolf Hess, the governor-general of occupied Polish territories Hans Frank, high-ranking SS member Ernst Kaltenbrunner, Foreign Minister Joachim von

Ribbentrop, Albert Speer, Alfred Jodl, Julius Streicher and Martin Bormann (although it was later proved that he was dead, he was tried *in absentia*). Also on trial were the Reich cabinet, the leadership corps of the Nazi Party, the SS, the SA, the SD, the Gestapo and the General Staff and High Command of the German armed forces.

In the opening statement, US Supreme Court Justice Robert Jackson, the chief US prosecutor, said: 'In the prisoners' dock sit twenty-odd broken men. Reproached by the humiliation of those they have led almost as bitterly as by the desolation of those they have attacked, their personal capacity for evil is forever past. It is hard now to perceive in these men as captives the power by which as Nazi leaders they once dominated much of the world and terrified most of it. Merely as individuals, their fate is of little consequence...

'What makes this inquest significant is that these prisoners ... [are] living symbols of racial hatreds, of terrorism and violence, and of the arrogance and cruelty of power... Civilization can afford no compromise with the social forces which would gain renewed strength if we deal ambiguously or indecisively with the men in whom those forces now precariously survive.'

Using detailed information and a list of names of the individuals responsible for the specific crimes for which they were charged, compiled by the UN War Crimes Commission (UNWCC) with the cooperation of other members of the anti-Nazi alliance, as well as information concerning the 'extermination' of the Jews provided by various Jewish organizations, the prosecution commenced. The proceedings, which lasted almost a year, provided copious documentary evidence of unprecedented cruelty and inhumanity in the conduct of Nazi Germany. Indictments included conspiracy to

Max Faust (l), chief engineer of IG-Farben, the chemicals firm that produced Zyklon B for the gas chambers, with Heinrich Himmler, head of the SS, on a visit to Auschwitz at the beginning of the 1940s.

plan, initiate and wage wars of aggression, and war crimes such as the invasion of Poland and massacres in France, Belgium, Germany, Italy, Greece, Czechoslovakia and Serbia. Both the Americans and the Russians screened footage shot by Allied filmmakers in liberated areas that showed graphic details of atrocities. There was much interest, too, in the genocide of Jews in German-occupied Europe, which had become known as the Shoah or the Holocaust. Hundreds of documents and witnesses referred to the persecution and suffering of the Jews, while an SS officer and Rudolf Höss, the commandant at Auschwitz, gave evidence about the origins of the Final Solution. A notable contribution came from the French journalist Marie-Claude Vaillant-Couturier, who provided an eyewitness account of the brutality at Auschwitz where she spent three years.

Her testimony included the following descriptions: 'We saw the unsealing of the cars and the soldiers letting men, women, and children out of them. We then witnessed heart-rending scenes; old couples forced to part from each other, mothers made to abandon their young daughters, since the latter were sent to the camp, whereas mothers and children were sent to the gas chambers. All these people were unaware of the fate awaiting them… They were taken to a red brick building, which bore the letters "Baden", that is to say "Baths". There, to begin with, they were made to undress and given a towel before they went into the so-called shower room . . . gas capsules were thrown through an opening in the ceiling. An SS man would watch the effect produced through a porthole. At the end of 5 or 7 minutes, when the gas had completed its work, he gave the signal to open the doors; and men with gas masks – they too were internees – went into the room and removed the corpses. They told us that the internees must have suffered before dying, because they were closely clinging to one another and it was very difficult to separate them. After that a special squad would come to pull out gold teeth and dentures; and again, when the bodies had been reduced to ashes, they would sift them in an attempt to recover the gold.'

The court adjourned on 1 September 1946.

Despite the differences in the preferred outcome of the trial of each of the Allied governments, the cracks had been papered over and the first punishments were handed out to those on trial when sentencing began on 30 September. In judgement, the court made it clear that it did not accept the defence many offered that they were 'merely following orders'. In his speech before sentencing, Lord Justice Geoffrey Lawrence, President of the Tribunal, said of the accused, 'They have been responsible in large measure for the miseries and suffering of millions of men, women and children... Without their military guidance the aggressive ambitions of Hitler and his fellow Nazis would have been academic and sterile . . . they were a ruthless and military caste... Many of these men have made a mockery of the soldier's oath of obedience to military orders. When it suits their defence they say they had to obey; when confronted with Hitler's brutal crimes which are shown to have been in their general knowledge, they say they disobeyed. The truth is that they actively participated in all these crimes or sat silent and acquiescent, witnessing the commission of crimes on a scale larger and more shocking than the world has ever had the misfortune to know.'

Twelve of the accused were sentenced to death (including Göring, Ribbentrop, Keitel, Kaltenbrunner, Jodl and Bormann); seven received prison sentences (of between 10 years to life imprisonment); three were acquitted and two were not charged. Ten of the death sentences were carried out on the night of 16 October in the gymnasium of the court building by hanging at the hands of the executioner, US Master Sergeant John C. Woods. Their bodies were cremated and the ashes disposed of in the Isar river. Of the other two, Göring committed suicide by ingesting cyanide in his cell the night before, and Martin Bormann was still listed as missing. The seven sentenced to incarceration were sent to Spandau Prison in Berlin.

With no television coverage and the public unable to be in the courtroom, the world's press played a huge part in reporting proceedings and interpreting the lessons to be learned from the conflict. Over 160 writers, artists, photographers and filmmakers meditated on and interpreted the various competing opinions of both the trial and the war itself. There were criticisms of the legitimacy of the trial (as Germany had not signed the London Charter), charges that the court simply handed out victors' justice, and concerns that the punishments were *ex-post facto* because the crimes were committed before the new laws were passed. On the other side were complaints that crimes committed before the outbreak of the war had not been included, that so few Nazis had been prosecuted, and that the punishments were somehow inadequate for such huge crimes. There were also claims that crimes carried out by the Allies had not been included, particularly during the Soviet invasion and occupation of Poland and the Allied bombing that obliterated cities such as Dresden, Cologne and Hamburg.

Despite this, the IMT trial was regarded as having satisfied the popular desire for retribution, and the rules it established are now regarded as the 'birth of [modern] international law', having informed, among other protocols, the UN Genocide Convention and the Universal Declaration of Human Rights (both 1948) and the Geneva Convention (1949), and as having initiated the establishment of the permanent International Criminal Court in 1998.

THE 'ZONAL' TRIALS

Although it was the most famous of all the World War II trials, the First Nuremberg Trial was not the first nor the last trial for crimes committed during the conflict. The four Allied powers, the US, Britain, France and the Soviet Union, held further trials in their zones of occupation, which had been ratified at the Potsdam Conference held following the end of hostilities. They were intended to try lower-level Nazi Party officials and functionaries. Many of the earliest 'zonal' trials, particularly in the US zone, involved the murders of Allied soldiers who had been captured by German or Axis troops. Trials in the US zone were held in the same Nuremberg courtroom as the IMT trial between December 1946 and April 1949, under the jurisdiction of the US military. In the British Zone of Occupation alone, 365 trials were held, involving more than 1,000 war criminals.

The trials included proceedings against leading industrialists, military figures, SS members and others. A number of the trials paid special attention to the intended annihilation of the Jews under the Nazi regime. The Pohl trial, for example, saw 18 Nazis, including Oswald Pohl, accused of crimes against inmates of the death camps. The *Einsatzgruppen* trial brought cases against SS and Gestapo members of Nazi 'death squads' who were responsible for murdering approximately one million Jews in conquered German territories in eastern Europe. The Doctors' Trial dealt with doctors and nurses who had participated in the killing of physically and mentally impaired Germans and who had performed medical experiments on people imprisoned in concentration camps (see Chapter 4). The final trial, known as the High Command Case, was presented with a Nazi document detailing the requests and approval of all Nazi Party and government institutions involved in the implementation of the Final Solution. All 127 of the Nazis on trial were found guilty. Of these, 12 were sentenced to death, 25 to life imprisonment and the rest to long prison sentences.

The US military also hosted a trial at Dachau where some

1,200 camp guards, SS units and medical personnel from Dachau itself and other camps in the area were tried for committing atrocities, executions, conducting medical experiments on camp inmates, the establishment and operation of gas chambers and participation in the Malmedy massacre in Belgium in December 1944 when 750 prisoners of war were executed. In all, 1,672 individuals were tried and 1,416 were convicted, with 297 sentenced to death by hanging, and 279 to life in prison.

In the British zone, there were trials at Lüneburg, Hamburg and Wuppertal. These trials differed from the American trials as the British only tried those accused of committing crimes against British subjects. Between them, British military tribunals brought charges against more than 1,000 defendants, including staff from the Bergen-Belsen concentration camp. Of the 45 defendants from Belsen, 11 – including the commandant Josef Kramer – were sentenced to death by hanging, while 14 were acquitted. Another trial put executives from Tesch & Stabenow – a company that manufactured Zyklon B, the poisonous gas used to kill Jews in the camps – in front of the British tribunal. Two of three defendants were sentenced to death.

For both the French and the Soviets, attitudes towards the post-war trials were shaped by the fear and horror of occupation. The French tried over 2,000 people, with 104 sentenced to death, though many of them were collaborators rather than war criminals. The Russian trials were even more dominated by retribution for the brutality of the war and occupation on the Eastern Front. As we have seen, Soviet war crimes trials began in 1943. There are no official figures available for the number of people tried by the Russians, but it is known that more than 13,000 soldiers were convicted in those early trials, and a further 15,000 suffered the same fate in the Soviet zone in the years after the war. Though many were executed, most of those convicted were in large measure deported to Soviet territories to serve their sentences. It is fair to say that the actual figures from the Soviet trials dwarfed those of the war crimes programmes of the other Allied powers.

WHO ELSE WAS GUILTY?

Trials were also held elsewhere in countries that had suffered German occupation and in those that had become part of the Axis, such as Hungary, Romania, Bulgaria and Yugoslavia. Some of the worst war crimes had taken place in Poland and the Baltic States, Ukraine and Belorussia. In Poland, where most of the Nazi death camps were situated, those present in the courtrooms heard terrible stories of torture and inhuman savagery that revealed acts of killing for pleasure at Auschwitz, Belzec, Treblinka, Majdanek, Sobibor, Chelmno and other camps across the country; estimates put the total number of deaths in these camps at somewhere around three million people. One of the most important trials was that of Rudolf Höss, the longest-serving Auschwitz commandant, who was tried by the Polish Supreme National Tribunal in Warsaw. He was sentenced to death, taken to the camp and executed by hanging in front of the crematorium. A second Auschwitz trial, at Krakow, issued a further 23 death sentences and 17 long prison terms.

Trials in the Soviet Union have been less well studied, partly because Soviet archives have been hard to access and partly because many of the tribunals were used as obvious propaganda vehicles. The trials, which began again in December 1945 in cities across the Soviet Union and its associated socialist states, were often well attended, and punishments, most likely by hanging, were popular public events in the years after the war. The trials concentrated on atrocities against Soviet civilians and POWs, a tactic that immediately nullified the defendants' claims to be prisoners of war. Tribunals paid particular attention to the Holocaust, especially if they were held in areas with substantial pre-war Jewish populations, such as Kiev in the Ukraine, Riga in Latvia and Minsk in Belorussia. Although the Soviet press still downplayed the Holocaust by pointedly referring to the murdered Jews as 'Soviet citizens', these trials became the first instances that revealed to the Soviet public the true scope of the Jewish tragedy.

The testament of Friedrich Jeckeln, SS commander for the Ukraine and the Baltic lands, was particularly revealing about the Nazi campaign against the Jews and Gypsies in the region. Hitler's wishes and Himmler's orders were to eliminate them all. In his testimony at the Riga Trial, Jeckeln admitted that it was his responsibility to carry out the order. He began by liquidating the Riga ghetto, ordering the *Einsatzkommandos* and police to murder between 20,000 and 25,000 Jews, including 8,000 children. By June 1942, 87,000 Jews in Latvia had been killed, many by gassing. It had been Nazi policy to deport Jews and Gypsies to this region for liquidation. Jeckeln was eventually charged with the complete extermination of 300,000 Soviet citizens of Jewish nationality in the Baltic area, as well as 200,000 in Belorussia.

Two Order Police generals also appeared at the Minsk Trial charged with the organization and killing of Jews in Minsk and Kiev, although they claimed to have been posted after most of the killing had taken place. Eberhard Herf recounted the horrors of the Minsk ghetto liquidation during which more than 80,000 Jews had been murdered, many with sadistic barbarity. Paul

Albert Scheer was able to shed light on the Babi Yar massacre in the Ukraine, one of the worst of the conflict. In retaliation for explosions that rocked the city of Kiev in September 1941, the entirety of the Jewish community was to be put to death. On 29 and 30 September, 33,771 people were machine-gunned and shot to death on the edge of a ravine. Their bodies were then covered with sand before the next batch of victims was brought in. They died naked, as their clothing, valuables and money were taken from them and distributed to the ethnic Germans living in the area. This was a key moment in the pursuit of the Final Solution, as Himmler realized that in order to finish the job, quicker methods of killing had to be found.

Trials took place elsewhere in Europe too: Belgium, the Netherlands, Czechoslovakia, Austria and in Germany itself. In December 1945, the Allies realized the importance of allowing German courts to reopen. The Allied Control Council Law No. 10 authorized the trying and sentencing of crimes committed during the war years by German citizens against other German nationals or stateless persons. The first cases pursued were concerned with the Nazi Euthanasia programme to kill people with mental and physical disabilities, where both victims and perpetrators were most likely to be German nationals.

Towards the end of 1949, the burning need for punishments against former Nazis began to abate, both inside and outside Europe. Trials in Britain, France, Australia, Canada and the US, for example, had become few and far between. Up to this time, the Nazi Leadership Corps, the Gestapo, the SA and the SS had borne the brunt of Allied justice, as was right because these were the principal instruments of Hitler's tyranny. It was they who perpetrated the mass murders in the concentration and death camps; the murder and ill-treatment of POWs and foreign workers in slave labour; the interrogations; the torture and the outlandish experiments on human guinea pigs.

Following the cessation of the 'denazification' programme in 1953 (see Chapter 5), interest in searching for former Nazis began to fade. Many took advantage of this, moving abroad, often to South America, and starting new lives. But interest in hunting Nazis never actually went away completely, and the subject would pop up in the world's conscience from time to time and, as we will see, is still very much alive today.

CHAPTER 4
NAZI DOCTORS

HITLER OUTLINED his core beliefs on race and the creation of a superior Aryan society in his book *Mein Kampf*, first published in 1925. By 1939, the book had been translated into 11 languages and sold more than five million copies. Influenced by discussions on Social Darwinism and eugenics in Germany in the pre- and post-war years, Hitler believed that interbreeding between different racial and ethnic groups was wrong and would hamper the development of the German 'master race', claiming that 'Blood mixture and the resultant drop in the racial level is the sole cause of the dying out of old cultures...' His ideas included the ranking of races into '*über*' and '*unter*' *menschen* (superior and inferior peoples) and the exploitation of one by the other. For him, this meant Aryan subordination of the inferior and weaker Jews, Gypsies, Slavs (Poles, Serbs, Russians) and others. It also included the physically and mentally disabled.

Once in power, Hitler began pursuing his racial policies in earnest, instigating a campaign to cleanse German society of those he regarded as biological threats to the nation's health. For this, he needed the collusion of health professionals of all kinds. From our viewpoint today, the idea that Nazi ideology could appeal to doctors and nurses is ridiculous. But, according to historians and sociologists, in the 1930s members of the medical profession were among the staunchest supporters of the Nazi regime. By 1945, 45 per cent of them had joined the Nazi Physicians League; in all, 7 per cent of doctors were SS members (compared with 0.5 per cent of the general population). There are several reasons put forward for this. Propaganda played a big part by accusing Jews of contaminating the nation's health and claiming that Jewish doctors, of which there were many, were blocking the promotion of German-born colleagues. As well as offering career opportunities, Nazi ideology had other appeals: with its emphasis on biology and research support, its vision of improving the genetic composition of Germany's citizenry in the hope of creating a society in which individuals would be economically useful was attractive and felt to be achievable by those who believed that they were at the 'cutting edge of science' at the time.

In *The Rise and Fall of the Third Reich*, author William Shirer described the Nazi doctors who went well beyond the boundaries of normal professional medicine as 'irrational psychopathic butchers', in an attempt to explain the horrors and atrocities for which they were responsible during their work in the concentration camps. In reality, many of them were expert physicians at the top of their fields. It seems likely that they were tempted by Nazi belief that certain 'races' were superior to others and that scientific management could solve social problems (preventing the propagation of the 'unfit'). There was also the conviction that mental illness justified compulsory sterilization and that the measure of individual worth should be in economic terms (according to Nazi doctrine, it was vital to reduce the cost of the 'defective' or non-productive population). After all, these beliefs simply reflected basic utilitarian moral principles.

Hitler's rise to power took advantage of the collapse of the economy in Germany in the years following World War I. Immediately after Hitler's appointment as chancellor in January 1933, the Nazi regime began to rule by fear. After a vigorous media campaign and the suspension of much legal protection, the new government focused that fear on the Jews. Bigotry and prejudice on the one hand, and the quest for knowledge unhindered by consideration of its source on the other, collaborated to create one of the cruellest episodes in medical history. According to an article in medical journal *The Lancet* in 2012, this included 350,000 coerced sterilizations, the euthanasia of 260,00 psychiatric patients, the practice of eugenics, race medicine, new marriage laws, the killing of children regarded as 'defective' and at least 25,000 experiments in concentration camps and on prisoners. It is estimated that at least 350 doctors were involved in these experiments. At least 2,000 people are known to have died, while thousands were permanently physically and mentally impaired as a result of the cruel and sadistic methods used on them. In addition, tens of thousands of the bodies of those executed in the camps were used for medical research and teaching.

The sketchy details of the scale of the operation of Nazi concentration camps and death camps were added to swiftly as the Allies began to liberate them in the early months of 1945. The Nuremberg Doctors' Trial provided the first public examination of conditions inside the camps and of the inhumane, pseudo-medical experiments carried out on thousands of inmates. The trial of 23 doctors, which began in December 1946, included the testimony of 85 witnesses and the examination of 1,500 documents. In their defence, the physicians argued that much of their work involved looking after the camps' staff and that anyway their crimes were not their fault, since they had received their orders from on high. They added that treating them as war criminals would be disastrous for the reputation of medical research and science, especially as what they had done was, in fact, useful. They also claimed that military necessity justified their torturous experiments, comparing their victims to collateral damage from Allied bombings. The defendants also cited similar forms of human experimentation that they said had taken place in the US, giving names and details, but this was ignored by the judges.

Some of the Nazi doctors' experiments, such as those involving high-altitude and hypothermia survival, the development of pharmaceutical compounds to fight contagious diseases like malaria, typhus, TB and so on, and others relating to fractures and other war wounds, did have legitimate scientific purposes. Others, such as those relating to the creation of a 'master race' and the sterilization of 'undesirables', did not. For the judges at the trial, the fact that the experiments were carried out without the patients' permission and with total disregard for their suffering or their survival meant that the doctors had violated the rules of medical ethics. Of the doctors on trial, seven were sentenced to death, nine to long prison terms and seven were acquitted.

THE ANGEL OF DEATH

Josef Mengele, the doctor most closely associated with the appalling medical experiments carried out in the concentration camps without patients' consent, represents the dichotomy

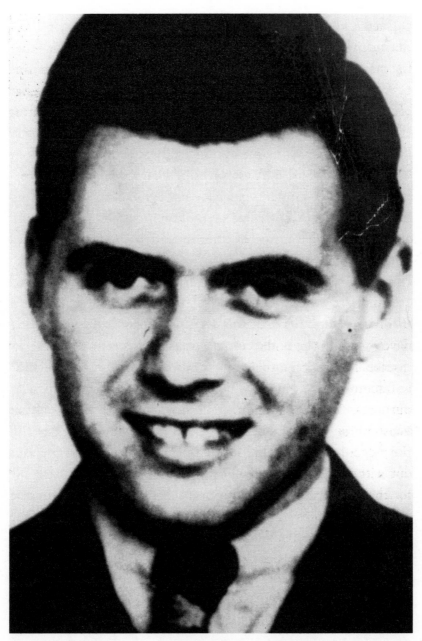

Josef Mengele, before he became known as 'The Angel of Death' for his activities in Nazi death camps. The picture was taken around 1940.

perfectly. He thought of himself as a serious scientist, and his son reported that when Mengele left Auschwitz in 1945, fleeing for his life as the Red Army approached, he took the results of his experiments with him, still imagining that they would bring him scientific honour. This is the same man described as follows in the dissecting room at Auschwitz by his 'assistant' Miklos Nyiszli, a Romanian physician picked out of the line by Mengele on arrival because of his skills at carrying out post-mortems: 'This was where he felt best! From here one could see the burning pyres. Here the smoke rose from the crematorium chimneys. Here the walls reverberated with the screams of those being murdered and the sound of the murderers' guns. Here Dr Mengele retired after every selection and every blood execution. Owing to his deranged "scientific" mania, he spent all his free time here, in this terrible atmosphere, instructing me to open up the bodies of hundreds of innocent victims.'

Born in Bavaria into a prosperous family in 1911, Mengele's upbringing was conservative and Catholic, but imbued with the anti-Semitism common to the time and place. A student of anthropology and genetic medicine, he joined the Nazi Party in 1937 and the SS in 1938, having become a believer in the idea of German racial hygiene.

He was drafted into the army in 1940, serving in the Waffen-SS. It is reported that his unit, the SS Fifth Armoured Division, was involved in atrocities against Jews in the Ukraine, and it seems likely that he witnessed extreme violence against soldiers and civilians, perhaps becoming inured to it. Promoted to SS captain in April 1943, he was posted to Auschwitz the following month as a physician at the Auschwitz-Birkenau Gypsy camp. In August the following year, the 4,500 inhabitants of the Gypsy camp were annihilated in the gas chambers and burned. Mengele then became chief physician at Birkenau (Auschwitz II).

As well as his 'medical' work, Mengele was in charge of selection. Whenever a train arrived at Auschwitz, those inside the boxcars were let out on 'the ramp', clutching their worldly belongings and each other. First ordered to leave their luggage, they were then divided into two lines by SS *Hauptsturmführer* Mengele: those on the right were destined to go to the slave labour camp; those on the left to the gas chambers. It is estimated that Mengele sent 400,000 Jews to their deaths between 1943 and 1945.

Anxious to make a name for himself in the field of medicine, Mengele wanted to search for the secrets of heredity. According to Nazi doctrine, the future of Germany could benefit from the help of genetics. If so-called Aryan women could give birth to twins who were sure to be blond and blue-eyed, the future could be saved. In the first phase of his experiments, Mengele subjected pairs of twins and people with physical handicaps to special medical examinations that could be carried out on the living organism. Painful and exhausting, these examinations lasted for hours and were a difficult experience for starved, terrified children. Subjects were photographed, plaster casts were made of their teeth and jaws, and their fingerprints and toeprints were taken. As soon as the examinations of a given pair of twins were finished, Mengele ordered them to be killed by phenol injection, so that he could conduct comparative analysis of internal organs by autopsy. Scientifically interesting anatomical specimens were preserved and shipped to the Institute in Berlin-Dahlem for more detailed examination. He had other areas of interest, too, and carried out experiments on women pregnant with twins, in dwarfism, the treatment of noma – a type of gangrene of the mouth common in Gypsies – during which he sawed off the heads of infected prisoners and sent the preserved samples to Germany for study. Although he was not an ophthalmologist, he became fascinated by the phenomenon of people with different coloured eyes, as he tried to discover a method for producing Aryan blue eyes.

On 17 January 1945, Mengele left Auschwitz and transferred to Gross-Rosen concentration camp in Lower Silesia (now in Poland), taking with him two boxes of specimens and the records of his experiments at Auschwitz (see Chapter 10). Two weeks later, the camp was liberated by the Red Army and details of the true horrors that had taken place there began to leak out.

FROM HEALTH TO HELL

Hohenlychen Sanatorium opened in 1902 as one small residential block with 30 beds and rudimentary facilities. It took children suffering from tuberculosis out of Berlin 50 miles to the south and offered them abundant fresh air in a landscape of lakes, pine forests and leafy beech woods. By the 1920s, it had developed into a renowned health complex with over 500 guest rooms and specialist centres treating a range of ailments. Its romantic setting of half-timbered fairytale buildings by the shore of Lake Zenssee attracted international celebrities throughout the inter-war years. Royalty, film stars and politicians all took advantage of the seclusion and the unsurpassed medical care that was available there.

In the early years of the Third Reich, Hohenlychen increasingly specialized in the novel concept of sports medicine. The German world champion boxer Max Schmeling trained for his comeback bouts there in the mid-1930s. In the run-up to the 1936 Olympiad, the German team made its final preparations for victory in the clinic's gymnasiums, swimming pools and extensive grounds. Even Jesse Owens made a pilgrimage there to have some repair work done on his knee cartilage. His surgeon was Dr Karl Gebhardt, the leading sports physician in Europe at the time, a man who had the honour of being senior medical officer for the Berlin Games. He had founded the sports clinic at Hohenlychen and pioneered new methods in orthopaedic surgery and rehabilitation. By 1945, however, Gebhardt would be notorious for the horrendous medical abuses that he supervised both at Hohenlychen and just a few miles away at the concentration camp for women at Ravensbrück.

In 1940, Gebhardt held several senior positions in the medical establishment of the Third Reich, notably serving as chief surgeon of the SS. Through his friendship with Himmler, he also enjoyed the confidence of many members of the Nazi top brass. But everything he had achieved was threatened in 1942 by his mishandling of a very special patient, the head of Reich security, Reinhard Heydrich. On 27 May, the Nazi Protector of Bohemia and Moravia was seriously wounded when an anti-tank grenade was thrown at his car by Czech partisans. Although two German surgeons on duty in Prague quickly managed to stabilize Heydrich's condition, Gebhardt was sent by Himmler to take control of the situation. Six days after the attack, Heydrich seemed to be making a good recovery. Gebhardt was claiming all the credit, refusing help from other senior Nazi medics, including Hitler's personal physician, Theo Morell. He ignored Morell's suggestion to try the new antibiotic drug sulfonamide, putting his faith instead in the traditional treatment of morphine and attentive nursing. Unfortunately for Gebhardt, the bomb that had destroyed Heydrich's Mercedes 320 convertible had blasted pieces of the car's upholstery, containing horse hair, deep into his stomach. Sepsis set in and Hitler's favourite faded away quickly and died on 4 June. Gebhardt was blamed. Despite this setback, he was determined to find a way to restore his reputation in the eyes of his powerful patrons.

THE RAVENSBRÜCK RABBITS

The women that Gebhardt needed came in groups of ten. Some arrived by truck; others were forced to travel the eight miles from Ravensbrück to Hohenlychen on foot. Once they arrived at the block fenced off from the rest of the complex, they met their new tormentors: Dr Fritz Fischer, formerly military surgeon to the elite SS regiment that served as the Führer's bodyguard; and Herta Oberheuser, physician to the League of German Maidens and a research specialist in dermatology with a keen interest in vivisection. She liked to call her mostly Polish victims 'rabbits'. Ludwig Stumpfegger, who later became Hitler's personal surgeon, served as Gebhardt's adjutant and made sure that the procedures were fully recorded.

In due course, the 'rabbits' were bound and prepared for the 'experiment'. Some of the women were lucky enough to be sedated; others were simply gagged or concussed. Deep incisions were then made along the length of their calf muscles. Some had their tibia or fibula snapped apart and the tissue surrounding the exposed bone gouged out. A range of contaminants were then introduced into their wounds. Various bacteria, random chemical solutions and mixtures of faeces and urine were injected into some of the 'rabbits'' limbs; others had pieces of splintered wood, shattered and ground glass, and strands of soiled fabric rubbed into their damaged flesh. Pus was sometimes introduced into the bloodstream to accelerate the rate of infection. Once the victims became ill from sepsis, differing quantities of sulfonamide were administered and the speed and effectiveness of the drug measured. Inevitably, many of the 'rabbits' subjected to these barbaric experiments perished: about a third died soon after their abuse. Most of the survivors suffered physical handicap and psychological trauma for the rest of their lives. In cases where the victims were deemed no longer viable, Dr Oberheuser was available to terminate their lives by injecting hexobarbital in an oil solution. She later claimed to be acting with humanitarian intent. Survivors remembered instead the pleasure that she took from watching the slow death of her still conscious, poisoned 'patients'.

Gebhardt and his colleagues later claimed that their obscene experiments during the summer of 1942 had a medical rationale. They were simply replicating the battlefield wounds that many German servicemen were routinely suffering at the Front. The real purpose of Gebhardt's experiments, however, was to discredit sulfonamide and justify the decisions he had taken in Prague several months before, and so win back the confidence of leading Nazis. His ploy was successful, his reputation was secured and further promotion followed. He continued to encourage distrust of antibiotics among his fellow military medics until the end of the war, badly weakening the Wehrmacht in the process.

RETRIBUTION

In May 1945, Gebhardt fled north towards the Danish border as part of Himmler's well-armed entourage. When he was arrested by the British, he was trying to reach Bremerhaven, where he hoped to board a ship bound for Portugal. His prominence during the Reich years and his particular closeness to Himmler were noted by the judges at the Doctors' Trial in Nuremberg. The judges were already horrified by Gebhardt's professional record, which turned out to have included crude attempts at attaching amputated limbs harvested from dying prisoners on to wounded German servicemen. Gebhardt was hanged at Landsberg Prison in 1948. His assistant Fritz Fischer was sentenced to life imprisonment in 1947. Fischer benefitted from the changed atmosphere in 1950s Germany. His sentence was first reduced to 15 years, but he was eventually released in 1954. He quickly built a new career within the pharmaceutical conglomerate Boehringer Ingelheim and lived to the ripe old age of 90.

Herta Oberheuser may have been callous and brutal towards her 'rabbits', but she presented a very different picture to the judges at Nuremberg when she stood in the dock, the only female charged with crimes against humanity in the Doctors' Trial. She made much of her femininity, arguing that no woman would have willingly carried out the monstrous crimes on her charge sheet. She had only participated in Gebhardt's ghastly experiments in the hope that her work might save the lives of young German soldiers. Sentenced to 20 years' imprisonment, she was released from Landsberg in 1952 because of her exemplary conduct.

Gebhardt's assiduous note-keeper, Ludwig Stumpfegger, was appointed resident medic at Hitler's HQ in East Prussia in October 1944. From then on, his destiny was linked to Hitler's: his last posting was to the Führerbunker in the heart of Berlin. He was killed alongside Martin Bormann, attempting to break through Soviet lines on the night of 1–2 May 1945. Their remains were found by construction workers in December 1972 and identified a few weeks later. Both skulls contained fragments of a glass capsule that had contained cyanide.

VILE EXPERIMENTS

Elsewhere in the Nazi war machine, another group of medics were busily engaged in research of dubious scientific value and appalling inhumanity. Unlike the sylvan setting enjoyed by Gebhardt and his associates, these Nazi practitioners undertook their murderous experimentation amid the misery of the prison camp built to hold Hitler's political enemies at Dachau, 20 miles north of Munich. Here, a number of doctors, some of international standing, busied themselves with examining three areas of medical and military interest: the impact of high altitude, low temperature and dehydration upon the human body. Like their colleagues at Hohenlychen, they were committed to the racial values of National Socialism and to the German war

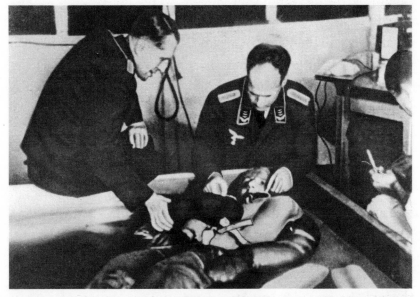

An inhuman hypothermia experiment conducted by Ernst Holzlöhner (l) and Sigmund Rascher on behalf of the Luftwaffe in Dachau concentration camp: human guinea pigs were forced to submerge for up to three hours in a tub of icy water, 1942–43.

effort. As a result, they felt empowered to treat the subjects of their research as less than human: mere *Untermenschen*. The cruel experiments at Dachau were of particular interest to the Luftwaffe High Command, which was acutely aware that it was engaged in a desperate war of numbers against the Allied air forces. It hoped that medical science could find ways to increase the survival rates of valuable, experienced aircrew who were often wounded in combat at high altitudes and faced with plummeting earthwards at high velocity in damaged aircraft. Moreover, it was already clear that the future of air warfare belonged to jet aircraft capable of operating at ever-higher altitudes. Any information that could be gleaned about human reactions in these conditions would be useful. Another Luftwaffe concern was the growing number of aircrew who were landing up and perishing in the cold, inhospitable waters of the Atlantic, the North Sea and the Baltic. After the disastrous early intervention of 'General Winter' – the nickname used to describe the deadly Soviet frosts – in the Russian campaign in late 1941, information about the physiological impact of extreme cold upon fighting men was also of interest to the Wehrmacht.

HIGH, LOW AND COLD

The plan to undertake a series of tests into the effects of high altitude and low temperature was originally the brainchild of Erich Hippke, general medical officer of the Luftwaffe. He found support for his ideas from Professor Ernst Holzlöhner of Kiel University, an academic, but more importantly also an officer in the SS. Much of the actual work at Dachau was organized and supervised by a Luftwaffe medic, Dr Sigmund Rascher, an ambitious member of the SS, whose research interests meshed with the aims of the project. Political support and the necessary money and resources came from Himmler. The SS Reichsführer also supplied the mostly Slav male prisoners who would be used, and murdered, in the course of the experiments. When their time came, they were taken to Barrack No. 5, which consisted of a pressure chamber and a dissection room. By reducing the pressure in the chamber, it was possible to simulate the conditions facing a pilot attempting to parachute from a damaged plane flying at extreme altitude. Raising the pressure level rapidly simulated the conditions experienced in freefall. The impact on the subject was usually lethal, but both the dead and the still living were subjected to immediate dissection in the adjacent room. Rascher claimed to have been looking to measure the impact of sudden pressure change upon the victim's heart, lungs and brains. Around 80 prisoners are known to have met their death in these tests between February and May 1942.

Rascher was also involved in the freezing experiments designed to identify ways of treating aircrew and troops suffering from hypothermia. Throughout August 1942, selected prisoners at Dachau were immersed in almost frozen water until near death; attempts were then made to revive them using water heated across a range of temperatures. Some doomed victims were 'revived' by being plunged into boiling water. Himmler took an interest in the project and thoughtfully supplied Rascher with four Romanian women from Ravensbrück; he wanted to see if the deeply chilled men might best be rewarmed by the natural 'animal warmth' generated by having naked women lie on either side of them. Before being released by the Luftwaffe in August 1943, Rascher had moved on to investigating ways of reducing the bleeding from gunshot wounds. By now viewed as psychotic in the eyes of many of his colleagues, his 'experiment' into the efficacy of one medicine thought to encourage blood to clot simply consisted of shooting a prisoner at close range and then administering a tablet.

HIMMLER HUMILIATED

Despite his high rank in the Nazi medical command structure and the fact that he had conceived and authorized the 'Luftwaffe' experiments, Erich Hippke managed to avoid the Doctors' Trial. Pleading illness and exhaustion, he resigned from his senior military posts in autumn 1944 and kept a low profile thereafter. He was only unearthed in December 1946 in Hamburg, where he was working as a locum GP and as works doctor for the city's underground rail company. He briefly appeared at Nuremberg, but as a witness for the prosecution. In the final years of his post-war career, he advised the West German air force on how to reconstruct and modernize its medical services.

Ernst Holzlöhner's unquestioning loyalty to the ideals of the NSDAP was rewarded when he was appointed rector of the University of Kiel in April 1945. But he had little time to enjoy his new position, as he spent much of the next two months being interrogated by Allied prosecutors about his activities at Dachau. Realizing that he was deeply implicated in the medical atrocities there, he took his own life in June rather than wait to be hanged by the British.

By then, Sigmund Rascher was already dead, executed not by the Allies but by the SS. His close friendship with Himmler had rested on the fact that he and his celebrity wife, a former singer and possibly ex-lover of Himmler, Karoline, had three young sons, all impeccably Aryan and all born when she was in her late 40s at least. The Raschers were living proof that the Nazi way of life, with its emphasis upon wellbeing, exercise and Germanic values, was healthy and fruitful. Unfortunately, this mirage evaporated when Frau Rascher was arrested at the main railway station in Munich, attempting to kidnap a small, male, blue-eyed infant. He was to be presented as the product of her fourth faked pregnancy. Himmler was humiliated and outraged. The Raschers spent the last months of their lives behind barbed wire. Karoline was hanged after trying to escape from Ravensbrück; Sigmund was shot by the SS in Dachau three days before the camp was liberated in late April 1945.

A HISTORY OF INFECTIONS

The German people understood the intimate connection between war and disease only too well. Popular folk memory recorded that infections took far more lives during the Thirty Years' War than all the foreign armies that rampaged through the land during the early years of the 17th century. German schoolmasters enjoyed horrifying their pupils with tales of the *Fleckfieber* or Spotted Fever epidemic in the winter of 1812–13: the freezing remnants of Napoleon's *Grande Armée* had donned the lice-ridden garments of their perished comrades and carried the infection into dozens of German towns as they struggled back towards France. During World War I, the German army in Russia and the Austrians in the Balkans both suffered heavy losses from typhus. The outbreak of typhus in Nazi-occupied Poland in 1941 and again within the Reich in autumn 1942 shocked Himmler, who was responsible for supplying enough healthy men for the German war effort. Accordingly, he urged the military to liaise with Germany's pharmaceutical companies and encouraged medical officers within the concentration camp system to make good use of the human resources at their disposal.

In December 1941, Dr Erwin Ding-Schuler was head of the Waffen-SS hygiene department and responsible for typhus research at Buchenwald, though he had little specific expertise in medical research. His promotion owed more to his reputation for loyalty and ardour as a member of the SS Death's Head division, plus his willing involvement in the murder of the troublesome oppositionist Pastor Paul Schneider in 1939. In fact, the experimentation that took place in Blocks 46 and 50 at Buchenwald was carried out by a group of selected prisoners with scientific backgrounds. The 'research findings' were collected, analysed and written up by Eugen Kogon, an exceptionally able Christian Socialist intellectual who spent the entire six years of the war as a prisoner in the camp. Ding-Schuler's role was simply to authorize the work and take the credit for the results.

During the winter of 1942–43, just under a thousand Buchenwald inmates were injected with typhus bacilli and then with untested vaccines. More than 600 of these disposable human guinea pigs died, and of the remainder most suffered long-term medical and neurological damage. In the last two years of the war, a number of research articles into typhus, typhoid and yellow fever appeared in the academic journals of the Reich. They bore Ding-Schuler's name but were actually written by the prisoner-scribe Kogon. Over time, an uneasy relationship developed between the two men that went beyond the norms of concentration camp regulations. They are known to have talked about everyday matters such as their pre-war lives, their families and, most dangerously, the future of Germany after the war. In the first days of April 1945, Ding-Schuler learned that Kogon's name was on an SS death list and he arranged for his 'colleague' to be smuggled out of the camp in a storage box. Ding-Schuler committed suicide in August during interrogation by US personnel. Eugen Kogon survived to become one of the great writers and thinkers who shaped the post-war idea of a united democratic Europe.

THE ENIGMATIC DR CLAUBERG

Throughout the years 1924 to 1939, there was little to suggest that Dr Carl Clauberg was an especially fanatical Nazi, or a cruel sadist. His thinking was influenced by contemporary beliefs in racialized eugenics, but that was still common in most advanced countries at the time. He became a member of the NSDAP after Hitler's rise to power in 1933, but that was obligatory for all professional citizens hoping to advance their career in totalitarian Germany. Clauberg quietly pursued a successful career in gynaecology and obstetrics, working at clinics within the universities of Kiel and Königsberg, publishing useful academic papers in his field that attracted some international attention, and devising a reliable procedure, the Clauberg Test, for measuring hormonal activity in women. As required, he joined the party organizations that supervised his profession of university professor, and he served as a first aider in a local Stormtrooper unit. Photographs of him depict a rotund, monkish man with an enigmatic smile.

His monstrous personal and professional transformation began in March 1941, when he was befriended by Heinrich Himmler. Since his days in Landsberg prison, Hitler had dreamed of creating a Greater German Reich stretching from the German Ocean, which the irritating British called the North Sea, to the western shores of the Caspian Sea on the very edge of Asia. The empire would embrace all the European peoples that Hitler believed had Germanic racial and cultural elements in their identity, such as the Alsatians, Flemish, Dutch, Danes and Norwegians. In the flat eastern plains that would soon be taken from the Soviet Union, the land would be repopulated by an Aryan elite of farmer-warriors, masters over the placid remnants of the Slav peoples. Events in Poland since the Blitzkrieg victory in 1939 were encouraging, showing how easy it was to decapitate and demoralize a nation by exterminating its intelligentsia and military leadership. Slavs would still be needed to fulfil their historic destiny as a servile underclass. However, it would be essential to limit their numbers strictly in line with economic requirements. And ways needed to be found to control their ability to breed, and so minimize their potential to pollute the racial purity of their Aryan masters. Clauberg's expertise in the field of fertility suddenly made him of great interest to the highest in the Reich.

STERILIZING THE SLAVS

Clauberg's job brief was simple and brutal: he was to develop feasible methods of rendering Slavic womanhood barren that were quicker and cheaper than surgery. And it was essential that the sterilization process should not reduce the labour value and efficiency of the women. Anything that he discovered would, of course, also be helpful in the ongoing campaign to eradicate the Hebrew race. Clauberg carried out his work at Birkenau and the central camp at Auschwitz, then at Ravensbrück, as the Red Army pushed west in 1944. His research programme involved injecting a series of acidic and caustic liquids into the uterus and ovaries of his subjects. After several applications, the inflamed, irritated tissue in the fallopian tubes melded and prevented the passage of sperm. To rule out the possibility of wasting time and resources on women who were naturally infertile, Clauberg selected married women with experience of several successful full-term pregnancies. Most of these mothers were Jewish or Romani. However, a number of virgin girls on the cusp of puberty were also used as a longer-term 'control group'.

These odious procedures were exceptionally painful and, for reasons of cost, were often carried out without anaesthetic. Approximately 700 women underwent these forced sterilizations, an unknown number of whom died from multiple organ failure. Most victims survived but were mutilated and traumatized for the rest of their lives. Some survivors were killed, so that full autopsies could be carried out and the affected tissues removed for further examination. Clauberg was also interested in the possibility of burning the ovaries of target women using excessive X-ray radiation, a technique actively pursued by several colleagues at Auschwitz. However, he favoured his own injection methods as they were cheaper, simpler and required no bulky, expensive and complicated equipment. In a joyful communiqué to Himmler, he boasted that a doctor with ten trained operatives could sterilize 1,000 'undesirable' women in one day.

After the war, it became clear that any ethical standards that Clauberg had maintained in his pre-war career had completely disintegrated during his time working at Block 30 Birkenau and Block 10 Auschwitz. To the physical and emotional pain that he inflicted upon his victims, he revelled in adding further layers of terror and humiliation. Survivors remembered his exceptional cruelty towards his frightened patients and the pleasure that he took in aggravating their fear and torment. He 'joked' with his subjects that after his experiments were complete, they would only be useful as pleasure women for the lowest and ugliest of the camp inmates. He confided to others that he had injected them with animal sperm and they were now carrying the foetus of a hybrid monster. As the Reich collapsed in 1945, Clauberg disappeared, but in early June he was scooped up by the Allies in a small fishing village close to the Danish border. He was eventually sentenced by the Soviet authorities to 25 years in prison for the murder of Soviet citizens at Auschwitz. Released in 1955 as part of the West German deal with the USSR, he tried to resurrect his career as a research gynaecologist at his old clinic in Kiel, but it was clear that he was now an alcoholic, deeply disturbed and behaving in 'abnormal ways'. He talked openly and proudly about his wartime activities, and publicly mocked the camp survivors who were demanding the withdrawal of his licence to practise and teach medicine. He died of a stroke in 1957 while facing renewed charges under West German law.

CURING HOMOSEXUALS

There was no place for homosexuality in the Nazi worldview. There had been a brief but limited flowering of gay culture in Weimar Berlin, but with Hitler's assumption of power in 1933, gay men were again persecuted and driven to hide who they were. The gay clubs and magazines of the 1920s were closed down. The old Romano-Christian law against 'unnatural fornication', known as Paragraph 175 in Bismarck's legal code, was enforced. In the 12 years of the Nazi Reich, more than 60,000 German men were incarcerated in prisons and concentration camps as punishment for their natural preferences. Gay German men had long been subject to the casual prejudice and discrimination that was commonplace in most Western societies of the period, but the Nazi oppression of homosexuality was motivated by much deeper political and ideological motives. The very foundation of the National Socialist nation was the traditional family unit, in which the fundamental duty of men and women was to procreate and thus ensure the health, progress and ultimate victory of the Germanic race. Nazi theorists with a simplistic, binary view of sexuality argued that homosexual men were abdicating their racial duty to contribute to the Volk.

Reichsführer Himmler was much vexed by the issue. He was aware that the loss of so many young men in the Great War was one cause of the disappointing number of German children born during the inter-war years. Germany was not breeding enough people to meet its economic and military needs, nor to fulfil its imperialistic goals. In his view, homosexuals, like Jews and communists, were another subterranean threat to the future of the German people. Himmler took comfort, however, in the prevailing popular belief that the condition was a disease, perhaps the result of hormonal imbalance. It could therefore be treated and cured, which is why he was keen to meet a Danish National Socialist, Dr Carl Peter Vaernet.

FRANKENSTEIN EXPERIMENTS

In late 1943, Vaernet and his family had moved to Berlin. Known to be an ardent Nazi, Vaernet's medical practice in Copenhagen had shrivelled during the German occupation of Denmark as patriotic Danes shunned his clinic. He was also under investigation for the illegal sale of morphine. Vaernet had studied hormone disorder as a student and had a hunch that homosexuality was caused by a lack of testosterone. His treatment turned out to be as crude as his ill-informed 'theory'. With support from Himmler and Ernst Grawitz, the head of SS physicians, Vaernet set to work at Buchenwald in June 1944 on his bizarre Frankenstein experiments. His reports record that he treated a total of 17 patients over the next five months. Most were homosexual, with several heterosexual men acting as a control group. Artificial 'glands' were inserted into the right-hand side of each man's groin. Some witnesses later remembered that the glands were metallic tubes; others spoke of Vaernet using bakelite capsules. The glands had a valve that drip-fed testosterone into the patient at regular intervals over several days. One witness remembered seeing Vaernet inject testosterone directly into a patient's testicles. In a report to Grawitz dated October 1944, Vaernet also reported that two men had been castrated and a third sterilized.

Two of the 17 men died, one from exhaustion, the other from infection, but both were really victims of botched surgery and appalling conditions. Unsurprisingly, Vaernet's surviving guinea pigs told him what he wanted to hear. The treatment had increased their self-confidence, increased their bodily strength and eradicated their homosexual urges, they claimed. Many of them had been imprisoned years before for being gay. They knew that giving Vaernet the correct answers was their best chance of escaping Buchenwald. In March 1945, Vaernet fled to Denmark, but his hopes of returning to a quiet life were dashed when his experiments were mentioned in a book about the horrors of the SS camps by Eugen Kogon, the prisoner-scribe assistant to Dr Erwin Ding-Schuler, the following year. Facing trial for war crimes, Vaernet feigned illness and vanished. He reappeared in 1947 as Carlos Pedro Varnet in Brazil, then moved to Argentina, finding a post at a medical institute in Buenos Aires, where he worked until his death in 1965.

MURDERING CHILDREN

Most Nazi doctors saw no contradiction or conflict between their calling as medics and their racial and political beliefs.

Using research subjects drawn from 'imperfect races' such as Slavs and Jews or the physically and mentally handicapped was not only morally acceptable, but provided the added bonus of helping to cleanse mankind of its regrettable impurities. The SS doctor Kurt Heissmeyer was typically steeped in Nazi racial theory. His work was designed to develop vaccines and treatments for infectious diseases such as tuberculosis, but also to find proof that they originated among the inferior races, as claimed by Nazi intellectuals. Throughout 1944, Russian prisoners at Neuengamme concentration camp, a short drive from Hamburg, were taken to a secret block where they were injected with tuberculosis. In many cases the mycobacterium was injected directly into the lungs. Victims who showed exaggerated or particularly interesting responses to the pathogen were hanged and then dissected by Heissmeyer and his colleagues in search of the evidence that fitted their beliefs.

In November that year, Heissmeyer repeated this procedure after taking delivery of a consignment of 20 Jewish children – 10 boys and 10 girls aged between 5 and 10 – from Auschwitz. As the British Army closed in on Hamburg, in an effort to hide the evidence of his experiments, Heissmeyer and his colleagues took the children and their carers to the basement of the Bullenhuser Damm school in the city, where they were injected with morphine and hanged.

The enormity of these crimes does not seem to have affected Heissmeyer, although he did put some distance between himself and the evidence that he left behind. He returned to his old home Saxony-Anhalt in the new Russian sector, working in his father's medical practice, before opening a prestigious private clinic for tuberculosis sufferers in Magdeburg. Justice only began to catch up with him in 1959 when he was mentioned in an article in the popular West German magazine *Stern*. Tried and found guilty in 1966, he was sentenced to life imprisonment in the infamous Bautzen II prison, notorious for its harsh regime under Nazi and communist governors. Heissmeyer lasted 14 months there before dying in his cell of a heart attack.

ENTRANCED BY THE NAZI DREAM

During 1945, the world was shocked by the images emerging from the ruins of the Nazi concentration and death camp system. Pictures of starving inmates on the edge of death, and the instruments of terror – barbed wire, guard towers, gas chambers, chimneys and spartan huts, more charnel houses than shelters, all became commonplace, as did photographs of the mountains of dead and the stunned faces of captured camp guards, silent and stupefied now that their horrendous crimes had been exposed.

One of the most chilling images captured in Germany year zero was one of the simplest, yet it illustrated the deep wells of evil that had fuelled and powered the SS extermination machine. Three men are in a pit of mangled, emaciated corpses. Two of them are scrambling on the slope of the pit, perhaps recognizing the body of a former campmate that they vaguely knew, or hoping to find in cold, clenched fingers a small trinket that the guards had failed to confiscate. The third man stands apart from them, perfectly poised in the centre of the shot. All three men wear simple shabby uniforms, fatigues that denote their status as prisoners. The presence of a British soldier at the brow of the pit with his rifle at the ready confirms that the men beneath him are a prison work detail. Yet the figure of the solitary prisoner in the middle of the slaughtered mess conveys nothing of defeat, guilt or repentance. His confident stance is openly defiant, legs outstretched and planted solidly with no care or respect for the bodies beneath his boots. Head unbowed, his gaze ignores the victims at his feet and casually disregards the guard behind him. This figure is far away in time and space, still entranced by the Nazi dream of ultimate victory and a hero's life in a world cleansed by the master race.

NECESSARY EVIL

The prisoner in the picture is Fritz Klein, an ethnic German from Romania. When war broke out in 1939, Klein joined the Romanian army as a lieutenant doctor but was delighted to be transferred to the Waffen-SS in 1943. He was posted to

War criminal Fritz Klein was a doctor at Auschwitz, Neuengamme and Bergen-Belsen. In 1945, he was forced by the British to bury the corpses of Nazi victims in mass graves. A few months later, he was executed.

Auschwitz-Birkenau, working in the sections devoted to women, families and Roma. His two main tasks were to minister to staff ailments and to act as selection officer, inspecting prisoners on arrival and identifying those too old, too weak and too young to be useful. Choosing those who were doomed for immediate extermination in the gas chambers was the primary task of the several hundred junior doctors within the system. Some, at least later, professed to have found these selection duties unpleasant, distasteful and regretful but, of course, they were a necessary evil if the German people were to enjoy racial health. Any doctors who refused to participate in selection duties were soon reminded by the SS of the strict penalties for those who betrayed the Nazi state. Fritz Klein did not need to be threatened. He relished the role of selection officer, which he saw as vital in bringing Hitler's vision to fruition. Klein was good at his job and he enjoyed it, although he later claimed he had never quite understood what happened to those who failed to meet the required standard of health.

As the Red Army ground its way westwards, Klein found himself working at camps in central Germany and was at Bergen-Belsen in Lower Saxony when British troops arrived on 15 April 1945. Most of the camp staff fled, but Klein remained at his post alongside his commandant, *Hauptsturmführer* Josef Kramer, to ensure an orderly handover to the Allied authorities. The British marched into a scene from a Bosch painting of Hell, with mounds of mouldering corpses at every turn; many of the living were so weak that rats gnawed at their flesh with impunity. Klein was given the task of digging pits and filling the mass graves with the 10,000 unburied dead lying around the camp. Nine days later, Sergeant Harry Oaks of the Fifth Army Film and Photographic Unit took the iconic photograph of Klein proudly standing among the men and women that he had helped to murder. At his interrogation, he expressed little guilt or remorse for his actions and did not try to implicate others. At his trial in autumn 1945, he repeated his conviction that he had acted both as a good doctor and a good National Socialist. Citing his own garbled version of the Hippocratic oath, he argued that the Jews were the gangrenous appendix of mankind: 'That's why I cut them out.' He made no mention of the oath's primary command, 'First, do no Harm'. He was hanged at Hamelin Prison by Albert Pierrepoint in December 1945.

CHAPTER 5

CIVILIAN GERMANY 1945—49

ON 23 May 1945, the German government, led by Hitler's successor Admiral Dönitz, was dissolved on the orders of the Allied supreme commander, General Eisenhower, marking the end of the Third Reich. Germany was now an occupied country. As victors, capitalist and communist allies shook hands in celebration of their triumph over fascism. For the civilian population of Germany, however, things were very different.

Their country was in ruins. Most of its cities had been reduced to rubble – 66 per cent of houses in Cologne had been destroyed and in Düsseldorf 93 per cent of buildings were said to be uninhabitable. An estimated 20 million Germans were homeless. There were no communication services and no working transport. The countryside, also mutilated by war, was populated by an estimated 5.2 million people. This included Germans attempting to return to homes that had been destroyed, evacuees returning to the cities having escaped the fighting on both Eastern and Western Fronts, former forced labourers of many different nationalities (known as displaced persons or DPs) returning home, as well as Germans returning from their former territories such as Czechoslovakia and Poland. According to a former head of the British German Department, it was 'as if a giant antheap had suddenly been disturbed'.

The economy had collapsed and there was no central government in place to implement instructions issued by occupying forces. Industry and agriculture were at a standstill, which resulted in a scarcity of food and the imminent danger of epidemics of disease. White flags hung from many of the houses still standing. Among the ruins of their country after a war that had cost some fifty million lives, the German people looked forward to an uncertain future.

WINNING THE PEACE?

After discussions at Yalta in February and then at Potsdam in July 1945, the Allies had agreed to divide Germany into four zones of occupation to be administered by Britain, France the Soviet Union and the United States. The city of Berlin was divided up in a similar way. Each zone was run more or less independently for the first two years of the occupation, although problems, policies, actions and results of occupation were similar in the British, French and US zones. In 1947, the British and US zones combined economically to form the 'Bizone', but they remained separate political entities.

On 8 May 1945, Field Marshall Montgomery had addressed his troops to mark Victory in Europe (VE) Day. He said, 'We have won the German war. Let us now win the peace.' British officials at the War Office had drawn up plans for the forthcoming occupation as early as October 1944. But soon after Montgomery was appointed commander-in-chief and military governor of the British zone of occupation, he realized that the directives were inappropriate for the reality of the situation his forces found on the ground. Immediate problems included the feeding, clothing and housing of the bewildered citizens of the defeated nation, and what to do with 1.5 million German POWs, a further million wounded soldiers and a similar number of refugees and DPs. Montgomery later recalled his thinking at the time, saying, 'I was a soldier and I had not been trained to handle anything of this nature... However, something had to be done, and done quickly.'

Montgomery and his deputy, General Brian Robertson, had some experience as members of an occupying force during the occupation of the Rhineland in 1918–19. They were determined to use the lessons they had learned then to avoid making the same mistakes. Committed to being positive towards their former enemies, they urgently needed to construct order from chaos. There were certainties: Germany had to be demilitarized, and industries controlled to prevent rearmament; law and order had to be restored, epidemics of disease avoided and economic activity restarted to prevent social unrest, but the task was huge.

Like all good soldiers, Montgomery approached the task of governing as though it was a military operation. Of course, safety was paramount: any weapons found were confiscated, strict curfews imposed and travel restricted. Named the 'Battle of the Winter', his operation was intended to address shortages of food, fuel and housing, and to repair water and sewerage works. He was also keen to restart economic and political life, to improve transport facilities, reopen schools and license political parties to prepare for elections. In June 1945, German POWs were released to take part in Operation Barleycorn, to bring in the harvest, and Operation Coalscuttle, to get coal mines back into production. Language was a barrier, as few of the British military authorities spoke German and few Germans spoke English. Progress was slow.

Another initial problem, particularly in towns and cities, was the clearing of tons of rubble from destroyed buildings, a task given over to the local population, particularly those who had been members of Nazi organizations. There were local resentments, as houses, villas and sometimes large areas of a city were requisitioned and the locals were turned out of their homes, creating serious anxiety for the newly homeless. The shortage of food continued to be a problem, with rations in the British zone, for example, of 1,000 calories a day for at least the first two years of peace. The British blamed this on the Soviets, who had demanded large-scale material reparations from defeated Germany. The Soviet zone of occupation, which included much of Germany's agricultural lands and was less populated than that of the other Allies, had agreed to supply food to the rest of Germany in return for a bigger share of reparations. But the food was not supplied, forcing the others to feed the population in their zones at their own expense. It proved costly, with British taxpayers footing a bill of £80 million in 1946–47.

Despite the problems, health levels remained acceptable, with none of the expected epidemics taking hold. British army engineers restored much of the transport infrastructure and the economy started to revive, but shortages of labour and raw materials meant that production remained low. Local political parties were licensed in late 1945. The British plan was to move from direct to indirect rule as soon as possible. Local elections were held in October 1946 for city, district and regional councils. Having initially tried to impose a British model of democracy, members of the new German parties convinced the British authorities that Germany had a strong tradition of local democracy better suited to its citizens.

PRISONERS OF PEACE

Between 1945 and 1949, the Allies arrested and interned some 350,000 suspected Nazis. They were housed in former army barracks, POW camps and sometimes former concentration camps, such as Buchenwald and Dachau. Conditions were poor and trials often chaotic. The situation varied in the different zones, with the British the most lenient and the Soviets the harshest. Many of those incarcerated in the Soviet zone were deported to the USSR as forced labour.

A similar but much bigger problem was presented by the millions of German POWs now the responsibility of the occupying forces, most of them in the west. In total, it is estimated that between five and seven million members of the Wehrmacht, the Waffen-SS and the *Volkssturm* were in captivity between May and July 1945. They were suffering from a shortage of food and shelter and insanitary conditions, as well as coping with the end of a war they had lost, which caused first shock, then worry and stress. However, those taken prisoner by the British, French and the US were more fortunate than those imprisoned by the Red Army. Large numbers of these prisoners were used as forced labour by the Allies, as had been agreed at the Yalta conference. In 1946, there were more than 400,000 German prisoners in Britain, there to perform agricultural work and for the purposes of political re-education. On the whole, they were well treated; at the end of 1947 when they were repatriated, some 24,000 chose to remain in Britain. In France, 740,000 prisoners, some in poor health, were used for work such as mine clearing. They were joined by at least 25,000 German citizens who had been expelled from their homes for acts of resistance against the occupation.

DENAZIFICATION

At the Potsdam Conference, the Big Four pledged to remove all traces of Nazism from Germany, agreeing that following its defeat the nation should be disarmed and demilitarized; its armed forces were to be demolished, and its population 'denazified' and re-educated. Their stated aim was to remove all Nazi officials from public life, and a list of suspected Nazis was drawn up for 'mandatory arrest'. But following the country's division into occupied zones, each of the occupying nations went about the task of denazification in its own way.

Of course, this was no easy task. As the German-Jewish writer Victor Klemperer wrote in 1946, 'Nazism had permeated the flesh and blood of the people through single words, idioms and sentence structures which were imposed on them in a million repetitions and been taken on board mechanically and unconsciously.' Many Germans had been brought up with Nazism and had it in their blood. The Party had sunk deep roots. In his book *The Scourge of the Swastika*, Lord Russell of Liverpool, a chief legal adviser at the Nuremberg trials, explained, 'From the Führer at the fountain source... The Gauleiter for the district, the *Kreisleiter* for the county, down to the *Blockleiter* who was responsible for some fifty households... the stream of Nazi doctrine flowed into every home. Each of these functionaries, at his own level, had a staff which dealt with every aspect of a citizen's life: education, propaganda, journalism, finance, justice.'

Allied attitudes towards the locals were not helped when the reality of the atrocities of the concentration camps and the death camps were made public. In fact, Allied commanders often forced the local inhabitants in nearby towns to visit the liberated camps so that they could witness the horrors for themselves, often being conscripted to bury the piles of emaciated corpses they found. In general, however, most German civilians were passive in their acceptance of the occupying soldiers. Shocked into submission, they seemed too preoccupied with their own private affairs to worry about the occupation.

Denazification also entailed renaming streets, parks, buildings, institutions and even children that had Nazi or militaristic associations. The authorities also had to remove monuments, statues, signs and emblems linked with Nazism or militarism, as well as confiscating Nazi Party property and eliminating Nazi propaganda from education by rewriting textbooks and altering the school curriculum, the German media and the many religious institutions which had pro-Nazi leaders and clergymen. They also had to prohibit Nazi or military parades, anthems and the public display of Nazi symbols. In the Soviet zone, many of the names were 'communized'.

Allied soldiers, former concentration camp prisoners and anti-Hitler Germans took their vengeance on Nazi symbols by burning or destroying swastika-emblazoned flags, banners and posters. In a moment captured on film, US soldiers blew up the huge swastika at the Nuremberg stadium, the site of former Nazi rallies. To those who witnessed it, whether in person or in newsreels shown in cinemas, the explosion symbolized the end of Nazism and the beginning of a new era. The Führer cult had to be discredited, and the former German leader was shown to have been a mass murderer whose policies had brought misery to millions of Europeans and led to the destruction of Germany. Film crews documented workers as they took sledgehammers to a massive metal bust of Hitler and melted down the lead printing plates for his autobiography, *Mein Kampf*, to produce type for a democratic newspaper for the new Germany.

The Allied occupiers handed out questionnaires to the local population in order to classify them in terms of the strength of their Nazism. If they were classed as Major Offenders, Offenders, Lesser Offenders or Followers, the intention was to punish them. Those not guilty of any association with the party were marked as Exonerated. Keen to teach their brand of democracy to the Germans, the Americans were strict in not allowing former Nazis to fill public posts. The British were less strict and more practical if the candidate was suitable for the post. The French were busy exploiting the resources of their zone to rebuild their own economy, so were completely flexible. For the Soviets, because their zone was to be turned into communist territory, anyone prepared to conform to that was allowed to remain in their post. By 1949, the denazification programme was turned over to the German authorities.

Through these actions, the Allies hoped to force German civilians to confront their recent past by demonstrating the criminality of the Nazi regime, either by the prosecution of the movement's leaders, by doing away with the trappings of the Führer cult and by discrediting the vestiges of Goebbels' propaganda, all of which had contributed to the regime's aggression, persecution and mass murder.

LEGACY OF HATE

During the last months of the war, Germany had been the scene of an orgy of killing, on the Eastern Front in particular, as the Red Army moved west and the German army retreated. Allies killed Germans; Germans killed Allies; Germans killed non-Germans; Nazis killed anyone not prepared to fight to the end; Allied bombing continued to kill German civilians, as did the epidemic of suicides that spread out across the country.

When the Third Reich collapsed, it left behind a legacy of hate and vengeance. This was greatly amplified by the discovery of the reality of the horrors of the concentration camps, where vengeance was often freely taken. Many people had suffered under the Nazi regime, not least German civilians, many of whom now turned the blame on their former authorities. Deep recriminations began to be voiced and were followed by the arrests of tens of thousands of former Party functionaries. The new authorities were inundated with denunciations of both high- and low-ranking members; some were real, others simply the result of petty local resentments. Whatever the reason, internment camps were needed for the thousands arrested and millions of Wehrmacht and Waffen-SS soldiers. Many of these were camps that the Nazis had used for Jews and other 'undesirables'.

As the months passed, however, and the effects of denazification began to be seen, although the arrests of important Nazis were still welcomed by the general population, enthusiasm for the rounding up of lower-level figures began to wane. As it was, fewer and fewer people were admitting to having held anything but contempt for the Nazis, and the arrest of those who hadn't really been responsible for any particular crimes implied that almost anyone could be taken into custody. Such was the rejection of the Nazi Party and its policies that it was hard to find anyone who admitted that they had once supported it. In his chronicle of the town of Tübingen near Stuttgart, in the French zone in 1945, German historian Hermann Werner noted: 'It was as if the National Socialist Party had disappeared from the face of the Earth . . . no longer was one aware of any preference for National Socialism. The petty Party functionaries who remained also overwhelmingly had had completely enough [of Nazism], again and again one heard from them that they, in fact, were the ones who had been cheated the most.'

In reality, many Nazis went unpunished and simply threw away their uniforms and returned to their normal lives and jobs. In her book *Reckonings: Legacies of Nazi Persecution and the Quest for Justice*, Mary Fulbrook, a professor of German history at University College London, makes some startling claims. She estimates that about 8.5 million Germans, about 10 per cent of the population, had been members of the Nazi Party, with many more enrolled in other related organizations, such as the German Labour Front, the National Socialist People's Welfare Organization, the League of German Women, the Hitler Youth and others. The Nazi state was run through these organizations, involving as many as 45 million Germans. Of the 200,000 involved in Nazi-era crimes, 140,000 were taken to court between 1946 and 2005, with 6,656 trials ending in convictions. 'It's way too late,' she said, following a trial in 2018, 'The vast majority of perpetrators got away with it.'

Although the Allied occupiers had been expecting to deal with fanatical Nazis, resentment, anger and reprisals, in fact they had encountered a defeated, confused and docile nation. Once the Nazi leadership had been dealt with, its main functionaries arrested and the army disbanded and interned in camps, the remaining population was compliant. They had been beaten into submission, by the war, by the Nazis and by the violence aimed at them during the last months of the war at the hands of invaders intent on taking revenge for the atrocities committed by German soldiers during the early years of the war. It bred a kind of collective self-pity, a victimhood, as though the German people felt they were taking the blame for the actions of others. They had been bombed into submission, with thousands of civilians killed and injured; they had also been forced in their millions to abandon their homes; hundreds of thousands of women had been raped by Soviet invaders, and now crimes perpetrated by their leaders had been laid at their doors. As historian Richard Bessel points out, 'The obvious injustice of this violence made the trauma of 1945 all the greater, and in the immediate post-war years made it easier for Germans to avoid facing what their nation had done to others, and to concentrate on what had been done to them.'

FEAR, SHAME AND GUILT
The start of World War II came 20 years after the end of World War I. Those years had been tumultuous for the German population, with defeat in the conflict and humiliation in the peace that followed. This period included the uncertainties of the Weimar Republic, the Depression, the arrival of Hitler, then economic revival and hope. When the Nazis took power, however, hope was replaced by fear. The fear was stoked by the propagandists, building up a terrifying picture of the barbaric, Bolshevik, 'subhuman' hordes. Those fears were justified in October 1944, when the Wehrmacht had driven the Red Army back from the East Prussian village of Nemmersdorf and discovered the remains of a massacre. Shocking photographs of dead children, and of women with rucked-up skirts and torn underwear, who had clearly been raped before death, were widely published. The intention was to stiffen German resolve. The actual result was that fear turned to panic.

Along with the fear came shame, particularly as Nazi actions became increasingly criminal towards the end of the war. As Hitler and the other Nazi leaders became even more frantic in their determination that everyone should fight to the death and indulge in their orgy of destruction, one faithful Nazi journalist wrote that, 'Everything I believed has turned out to be madness and crime.' Shame quickly turned to guilt as the truth about the appalling conditions in the labour camps and the bestial killings at the death camps at Chelmno, Belzec, Sobibor, Treblinka, Majdanek and Auschwitz-Birkenau became known. German historian Florian Huber notes that in the weeks following the end of the conflict, he heard the words, 'We didn't know. We didn't know', more frequently than any others. Of course, some people may not have known about the camps, but many did. As author Konnilyn Feig points out in her book *Hitler's Death Camps*, 'Hitler exterminated the Jews of Europe. But he did not do so alone. The task was so enormous, complex, time-consuming and mentally and economically demanding that it took the best efforts of millions of Germans... All spheres of life in Germany actively participated...'

However, the horrors were so unimaginable, the scale of the killings so enormous, that denial became an acceptable solution for the survivors. Take the example of Oskar Gröning, an SS officer at Auschwitz, interviewed by historian Laurence Rees in his book *Auschwitz: A New History*. 'In his office,' writes Rees, 'he [Gröning, charged with registering money taken from prisoners on arrival at the ramp] was insulated from the brutality, and when he was walking around the camp he could avert his eyes from anything that displeased him . . . he had nothing to do with the crude mechanics of the killing process – there was generally no reason for him to visit the remote corner of Birkenau where the murders took place.' In attempting to explain how he managed to tolerate taking part in what he knew was mass-scale murder, Rees explains, 'He shielded himself from taking responsibility for playing a part in the extermination process by constantly referring to the power of the propaganda to which he was exposed, and the effect on him of the ultra-nationalistic family atmosphere in which he grew up.' Even though Gröning never expressed guilt for his actions, he was haunted by the images in his memory. Around the time of his trial in 2015, he was approached for support by Holocaust deniers. In response, he said, 'I would like you to believe me. I saw the gas chambers. I saw the crematorium. I saw the open fires. I was on the ramp when the selections took place. I would like you to believe that these atrocities happened, because I was there.'

At the end of the 12 years of the Nazi regime, the majority of German civilians were desperate, tired of war and killing, and sorry for themselves. Catastrophic defeat left the entire nation suffering from emotional vulnerability after so easily being seduced into believing in the promises of a bright Nazi future. Fear, shame and guilt over how the Nazis had tried and failed to achieve this at such a colossal cost combined into a cocktail of feelings so toxic that it caused many thousands of Germans to commit suicide. For the survivors, it meant facing up to the truth.

COLD WAR ROOTS

Initially, the troops in the Soviet zone had the same concerns as the other Allies; they were liberating the concentration camps, clearing rubble and helping the locals find food, water and shelter.

But the Soviet military administration soon revealed different interests. Working closely with the German Communist Party, they set out – with similar concerns to the French – to ensure that Germany was never again going to be able to attack their country as well as to extract maximum reparations. They also began a campaign to introduce their ideology to German citizens in their zone, as well as in other eastern European nations behind what Churchill called 'the Iron Curtain', in a speech in 1946 – these included Czechoslovakia, Hungary and Poland, as well as Greece, Turkey and Iran.

As early as autumn 1945, it had become clear that the alliance between the Soviet Union and the other Allies was in danger of collapse. The Soviets were extracting everything they could from their zone: railway tracks, industrial machinery, even dismantling entire factories and transporting them back to Russia. They closed major German banks and insurance companies, seizing land and property. They showed an unwillingness to compromise or to do deals with the other occupying armies. As day-to-day cooperation deteriorated, matters came to a head, particularly concerning the Soviet responsibility for supplying food. In 1946, the Western powers, now keen to enable German industry to re-establish itself, refused to allow the Russians to continue looting its assets. Although a formal break between East and West was still in the future, opposing political sides were already forming. To combat Soviet expansionist initiatives, President Truman set out the position of the United States. In an address to the US Congress on 12 March 1947, later called the Truman Doctrine, he said, 'I believe that it must be the policy of the United States to support free peoples who are resisting attempted subjugation by armed insurgencies or by outside pressures. I believe that we must assist free people to work out their own destinies in their own way.' The battle lines for the Cold War had been drawn.

The split was also evident in the activities of the newly formed United Nations organization (UN), which had come into being in October 1945. Comprising 51 nations, with Britain, China, France, the Soviet Union and the United States as permanent members, its express wish was to prevent future generations suffering 'from the scourge of war'. In its charter, forged in the shadow of the nuclear bombs dropped by US forces on Japan in July and August that year, an act that started an arms race between the US and the Soviet Union, it was stated that decisions had to be unanimous; with the growing divergence of opinions between East and West, the Soviets began to make use of its power of veto, which compromised the UN's ability to do its intended job. Despite this, along with other newly created international institutions such as the World Bank and the International Monetary Fund (IMF), the UN began to help deal with the problems of refugees, rehabilitation and resettlement, as well as funding problems of major infrastructure resulting from the global conflict.

THE BERLIN AIRLIFT

Two years after the end of the war, much of Europe was still shambolic. The rebuilding of the infrastructures of a number of European countries, particularly Germany, France and Italy, had progressed slowly. For the Western Allies, this was concerning because of the growing strength of communist parties in these countries. With the confidence of the success of denazification, the Americans recognized the importance of bolstering the German economy and therefore its industry, not simply because it would help compromise communist influence but also because it would open up markets for American goods. They began to lay down plans to introduce currency reform to avoid the expected inflation caused by such a move.

By this time, many German politicians, economists, civil servants and other professionals had retaken their posts, particularly at a local level, and the occupiers were keen that they

A US C-47 cargo plane approaches Tempelhof Airport with food and other relief supplies during the Berlin Airlift, 1948.

took on some of the responsibilities by forming 'reconstruction' and 'anti-fascist' committees. Wilhelm Röpke, an economist on Germany's post-war currency reform council, suggested the creation of a new currency to replace the discredited Reichsmark. The Americans, realizing that the new currency would be stable and would end the threat of inflation, agreed, and on 21 June 1948 the Deutsche Mark was formerly adopted as the new currency of Germany.

In an effort to speed up the post-war recovery, US Secretary of State George C. Marshall announced the European Recovery Programme to provide significant financial assistance for the reconstruction of western and eastern Europe and the USSR in 1947. Enacted the following year, by 1951 it had provided more than $15 billion to help finance rebuilding efforts on the continent, reconstructing cities, industries and infrastructure, removing trade barriers between European neighbours and promoting commerce between European countries and the United States. In addition, however, it was also intended to halt the spread of communism on the European continent. Although countries in eastern Europe were invited to participate in the project and were earmarked as beneficiaries, Stalin refused to have anything to do with what became known as the Marshall Plan, blocking any potential aid to Eastern Bloc countries. Russian thinking was that the plan intended to 'enslave Europe and set it against Russia', explained Anatoly Semiriaga, an officer with the Soviet army in Berlin in 1945. In response to the Marshall Plan, the Russians created the Molotov Plan to provide help for the reconstruction of countries politically and economically aligned with the Soviet Union. It was a similar story with the North Atlantic Treaty Organization (NATO) in 1949 and the Warsaw Pact in 1955.

The first direct confrontation between the 'new' enemies came quickly. The Allies threatened to extend their currency reform into the Soviet section of Berlin; the Soviets refused. The Allies, who had merged their zones of occupation into a unified state in 1948, insisted. The Soviets, who had withdrawn from the four-power governing body in March, responded by blocking all access to Berlin in June, leaving the city – 100 kilometres (62 miles) inside the communist zone – as a capitalist outpost in hostile territory.

Stalin had been planning the blockade in advance, hoping to force the Western powers to hand the city to the USSR. The Soviets blocked all land transportation routes into and out of West Berlin, cutting off power and other supplies to its two million inhabitants. It had become a flashpoint, with the Soviets determined to starve West Berliners while the Allies, particularly the Americans, were determined to stay.

Wishing to avoid direct confrontation, in June 1948 President Truman ordered a massive airlift of supplies for West Berlin's beleaguered citizens. The aeroplanes and pilots that had been bombing the city a few years before were now helping to feed its inhabitants. The air corridor between Berlin and the West was the only remaining link and became its lifeline for the next 321 days as British and American planes landed roughly every ten minutes, bringing on average 4,500 tonnes of food, clothing, coal and other supplies each day. The city's two airports struggled to cope with the volume of air traffic, and a new one was built quickly with help from 1,900 local volunteers.

In a move designed to signal the seriousness of the situation to the Soviet Union, Truman sent a number of B-29 bombers – the only planes capable of carrying atomic bombs – to the region. Thus warned and sensing that the airlift could continue indefinitely, the Russians lifted the blockade in May 1949. It had been a PR disaster for them, as the forbearance and endurance of the people of Berlin illustrated their preference for a future with Western values.

THE DIVISION OF GERMANY

The other three powers had not been idle. In April 1948, they met in London to discuss the future of the territory of the Western-occupied zones, which included the 'city' of West Berlin. They decided to establish a constituent assembly, called the German Parliamentary Council, made up of representatives from the federal states (the *Länder*), which were based on pre-existing boundary lines. The council elected Konrad Adenauer, a Christian Democrat, as leader, and formulated what was the provisional constitution of the new Federal Republic of Germany (FRG). Bonn was chosen as the capital of the 'new' country, informally known as West Germany. The Federal Republic, which included the 'city' of West Berlin (still officially occupied by Allied troops), was declared to have 'the full authority of a sovereign state' on 23 May 1949, and aimed to be recognized as the rightful heir to the German Reich, but with the right of supervision retained by the Western Allied powers.

In response, on 7 October, the German Democratic Republic (GDR) or *Deutsche Demokratische Republik* (DDR) was established in the Soviet Zone, with East Berlin as its capital. A communist, Wilhelm Pieck, became president, and Otto Grotewohl, a former Social Democrat, was made head of government. However, the real power was held by Stalinist Walter Ulbricht. In 1946, the Social Democrat and the Communist parties had been forced to merge into the Socialist Unity Party, of which Ulbricht was the leader.

These actions marked the end of any possibility of a reunified Germany. For the next 40 years, East and West Germany served as symbols of a divided world and of the Cold War animosities between the Soviet Union and the United States that had begun during the course of World War II.

CHAPTER 6

THE RATLINES

ACCORDING TO historian Ian Kershaw, authoritarian regimes usually end in one of two ways: either because of some sort of revolution from below, or by some coup d'état or putsch from within the leadership. It was, however, impossible that the Third Reich could have ended in either of these ways. The oppressive authoritarianism of the Nazi regime bred such fear and moved with such pace that there was never the time nor the will to plot revolution from below.

In terms of the leadership, the failure of Claus von Stauffenberg's attempted coup in 1944, the brutality with which it was dealt and the fact that those Nazis at the top table, Bormann, Göring, Goebbels and others, were all set against each other, meant they were all currying favour with the Führer in the hope of personal advancement and too busy to plot against him.

At the top level of the Party, there were those ready to do Hitler's bidding and fight to the death: genuine fanatics, for whom 'death with honour' was better than defeat. Others were sanguine enough to know what they had done and admit to themselves that they had no future once the regime was over.

Discipline among the soldiers on the two fronts remained high, particularly among the Waffen-SS, but also in the Wehrmacht. For the lower levels of party leadership, the Gestapo, the SS, those responsible for the concentration camps and those not prepared to die for the cause, the choices were wider but, in some ways, harder to make. Many of them had been making their plans to escape retribution even before the war was over. They could stay at home and take their chances, they could hide out in Germany, maybe with new identities, or they could escape completely, get away, go abroad and find somewhere safe to live new lives. The more senior they had been, whether they had committed atrocities or not, the greater the need to escape. The Allies arrived in Germany with lists of those wanted for war crimes, and arrests began immediately. The situation in Germany was chaotic, with millions of people on the move; no one knew what was happening and no one was in control. There was no time to waste for those wanting to escape justice.

In no time, it seemed, escape routes opened up. Known as 'ratlines', so-named after crude rope-ladder rungs which allowed sailors on old square-rigged sailing ships to scale masts often in a last-gasp attempt to avoid drowning on sinking vessels, these were routes that led southwards out of Germany and Austria on to Italy or Spain, and very often on again to South America, the United States and the Middle East, among a whole range of destinations. The routes were organized by various networks of Nazi sympathizers, institutions and governments that all had an interest in helping them escape. One such institution was the Catholic Church and, according to some historians, the Vatican itself. There were several passes and valleys that led over or through the mountains. Most routes began in Innsbruck in Austria, where there was an office of the

International Committee of the Red Cross that may have been able to issue fugitives with an identity card. One route went through the spa town of Nauders in North Tyrol and over the Reschen Pass, another through the Ziller and Ahrn valleys to Bolzano, but the most important one was over the Brenner Pass. All routes led across the Italian border.

THE EMERGENCY EXIT

In the upper valleys of the Alps, good land had always been scarce and the growing season was short. Like highland farmers throughout history, therefore, mountain people made up their income by carrying goods from one side of the high ranges to the other, whenever a commodity was scarce, in demand or highly taxed. In the border lands between Austria and Italy, smuggling was rife for centuries. Local guides knew the best paths to avoid detection and also the right people to know and to avoid. They knew which villagers could be trusted and which officials could be bribed. For centuries, smuggling networks, based on family and neighbourhood links, passed on valuable commodities – livestock, metals and exotic foodstufs such as coffee – from one village to the next, out of sight of the government taxmen huddled in their customs posts along the roads far below. During World War II, smugglers in the Italian province of Venezia Tridentina, known by most of its inhabitants as Süd or South Tyrol, were busy carrying medicines northwards into Germany and bringing out currency and bullion. From 1944 until the early 1950s, their busiest traffic was in people, some Jewish, many German, but all looking to reach Italy and then move on to a new life elsewhere. Holocaust survivor and renowned Nazi hunter Simon Wiesenthal later wrote about this: 'I know a small inn near Meran where every now and then, illegal Nazi transports and illegal Jewish transports spent the night under the same roof without knowing about each other. The Jews were hidden on the second floor and instructed not to stir; and the Nazis on the ground floor were urgently warned not to let themselves be seen outside the establishment.'

Escaping Nazis received a warm welcome in South Tyrol and often stayed in the area for a while, perhaps in Bolzano or Bressanone, where Bishop Johannes Baptist Geisler threw open church properties and monasteries to shelter them, or in private homes or hospitals in Termeno, where the mayor was happy to hand out the residence permits needed to get ID cards, or in the spa town of Meran, known at the time as an 'El Dorado' for SS and other Nazi leaders. Once safely in South Tyrol, there were various underground organizations that took care of escaping Nazis and POWs, helping them to find safe lodgings. Conveniently, the region had also been a base for wartime forgers who were still equipped to provide them with fake papers. Once in possession of these, they could apply for an official passport from the Red Cross in Genoa or Rome.

The number of refugees who streamed down through the Alpine passes that ran from the Germanic lands into north-eastern Italy during the mid- to late-1940s is not known, but estimates range from 400,000 to well over a million. What is certain is that this constant wave of migrants contained thousands of men and women who were war criminals, and that everyone involved in their flight from justice knew this.

The route to Italy through South Tyrol became the preferred emergency exit for many senior Nazis for several reasons. By the last few final weeks of the war, the remaining cadres of the Nazi Party, SS and Wehrmacht were gathered in three clusters. Those in the east, in Bohemia and Moravia, were cut off from the west by the American and Soviet armies. Those in Schleswig-Holstein in the north were surrounded by the British, and there was no clear escape path through liberated Norway and Denmark or via neutral Sweden. With Allied forces blocking the way west, the only feasible escape route was south. A significant German force remained in Bavaria in the last days of the war. A number of SS and army units had made their way there, believing that preparations were being made for a final battle for the Third Reich that would be fought in the Alpine Fortress. Some were loyal fanatics who were willing to die for the cause. Most used the fantasy of an apocalyptic last stand to position themselves close to the Reich's border with Italy. And German fugitives planning to try their luck in South Tyrol knew that it was one of the few places where they could expect to find shelter and support in western Europe in 1945. As such, pretty much all that was left of the Third Reich was located here by the end of April that year.

Although a province of Italy for most of the 20th century, South Tyrol had been part of the German world for most of its history. Since the Middle Ages, the land had been ruled by German and Austrian lords and mostly populated by German speakers. In 1915, however, the secret Treaty of London promised the South Tyrol to Italy as a reward for joining the war on the Allied side. That promise was delivered at the Paris Peace Conference, and in September 1919 this essentially Teutonic region found itself governed by distant Rome. When Mussolini came to power a few years later, German culture in South Tyrol was suppressed. South Tyrol was to be Italianized. It was illegal to use German in official life or in schools. German newspapers were closed. Key jobs in the police and the administration went to reliable incomers from the peninsula. Squads of fascist blackshirts disrupted meetings of local people who protested or tried to maintain regional traditions. Inevitably, after 1933, the German-speaking South Tyroleans looked to Hitler to liberate them from Roman tyranny. The Führer's alliance with Mussolini postponed that outcome, but in a referendum held in October 1939 to settle the South Tyrol question, 85 per cent voted to become German citizens. In the chaos that followed Italy's departure from World War II, German forces took possession of the area in September 1943. For the next 19 months, South Tyrol was effectively ruled by the German army, police and the SS. Many aspiring fugitives made their plans for the future: routes were worked out, contacts made, assets transferred and spirited away. Even senior members of the Nazi elite arranged to get their families out via this region, including Hermann Göring's wife Emmy and Martin Bormann's family.

The area was occupied by Allied troops for the second half of 1945, but their efforts at enforcing security were chaotic and few Germans were turned over to the authorities; even regular Wehrmacht soldiers were confident enough to hide there. In December, the troops pulled out and South Tyrol became the first German-speaking region no longer under occupation, making the area even more attractive for Nazis and SS members still hiding in Germany and Austria.

PAPERS, PORTS AND BEYOND

Once over the border into northern Italy, escapees faced new challenges. They joined millions of others on the move: those who had escaped from territory occupied by the Red Army, POWs, displaced persons (DPs), survivors of the concentration camps and so on, all trying to find their way home or to find a new one. Favoured destinations were southern Italy, in particular Rome, Italian ports such as Genoa, and Spain, in particular Barcelona. In order to travel safely, it was necessary to have documents, especially proof of identity and, if necessary, travel documents.

Help was at hand for those who had not already acquired these in South Tyrol, both officially because the Italian government wanted people out of the country, and unofficially via the International Red Cross for humanitarian reasons. In addition, the Catholic Church and the Vatican wanted to help 'anti-communists' flee the Soviets. DPs were protected by the United Nations and could apply to the Red Cross for identity cards; holders of these cards could travel anywhere. Those without passports or those of unresolved nationality could also acquire new passports from the Red Cross, with the added advantage of registering them in any name. Especially attractive was the fact that photos on the passports had no imprint and were easy to change.

The system was open to abuse. The Red Cross sent thousands of blank passes to its offices in Rome and Genoa, which required only superficial identity checks for applicants. Nazis were able to obtain affidavits for these passes from church organizations that were officially supposed to be assisting refugees from Catholic countries. The Austrian historian Gerald Steinacher has provided evidence of Vatican complicity in this, claiming that the papal secretary of state Giovanni Montini, later to become Pope Paul VI, permitted the running of aid committees in Rome by Bishop Alois Hudal and Monsignor Krunoslav Draganović that were used by fleeing Nazis and their collaborators (see Chapter 7). In return, many SS men allowed themselves to be rebaptised. Steinacher argues that this was part of a Vatican strategy to re-Christianize Europe.

One of the earliest ratlines was to Spain. Although Spain had remained nominally an independent country during World War II, it had close ties with Germany. Hitler supplied troops and military hardware that helped the fascist dictatorship of General Franco win the Spanish Civil War in 1939 against the 'communist' Republican government. An agreement signed between General Martínez Anido and Heinrich Himmler in July that year revealed shared goals in rooting out communists and other subversive elements, which explains why the Nazis deported some 10,000 Spanish refugees – who had fled to France in fear of Franco's new regime – to concentration camps in Germany. The shared goals are also revealed by the list of names of 6,000 Jews drawn up by the Franco regime and 'presumably given to Himmler', according to the newspaper *El País*. Connections between the Nazi and Franco regimes continued to grow, with some 350 Spanish firms, controlled by a holding company called Sofindus, secretly supplying the German military. Their most important product was tungsten – mined in Galicia, and used to harden the armour of German tanks – the sale of which brought in much needed funds to the Spanish economy.

Support for the Nazis in Spain also came from the Catholic Church, often with the collusion of the Vatican. Republican forces had been responsible for the deaths of hundreds of priests and nuns during the Spanish conflict; the legacy of this was not necessarily love of the Nazis but fear of communists. For some of those crossing the border into northern Italy or eastern France, Spain was an attractive destination. It offered a safe haven for those who wanted to live there, and safe routes out of its ports to Argentina and other South American destinations. Both Charles Lesca, a member of the right-wing Action Française, and Pierre Daye, a Belgian Nazi collaborator, made the journey successfully with the help of Argentine cardinal Antonio Caggiano – Lesca to Uruguay and Daye to Argentina – and subsequently organized the ratline for others. The route even earned a nickname, *Das Trampolin*, because from here Nazis were sprung across the Atlantic to friendly South American countries. But many stayed on the peninsula. By 1946, it is estimated that there were hundreds of war criminals and thousands of Nazis and fascists in Spain, many living in safety and comfort in Barcelona, Madrid and, later, in Denia on the Costa Blanca.

In 1998, *El País* journalist José María Irujo searched Spanish government files and unearthed a list of 104 Nazis living in Spain just after the war, along with evidence that they were shielded by the Spanish government and tipped off about any possible searches. He found evidence of a further 600 Nazis who had chosen to stay, such as Otto Remer, an SS general, and Leon DeGrelle, a former leader of the Waffen-SS who had made it there despite facing the death sentence in his native Belgium.

Even after Franco's death and the restoration of democracy in 1975, the new socialist government continued to block efforts to bring Nazi war criminals to justice, claiming that it was important that Spaniards wanted to put everything related to the dictatorship behind them to ease reconciliation efforts. Irujo's investigation put the lie to Spain's apparent neutrality in World War II, painting it instead in the guise of a collaborator state.

THE ROMAN WAY

Those lucky enough to have procured the necessary papers, passports and travel visas in South Tyrol – such as Josef Schwammberger, the sadistic labour camp commander in Nazi-

Fanatical anti-Semite Adolf Eichmann was asked by Reinhard Heydrich to help manage the mass deportation of Jews to concentration camps. He was more than happy to oblige.

occupied Poland, Adolf Eichmann, 'architect of the Holocaust', and Dr Josef Mengele – went directly to Genoa, probably via Verona, where they boarded ships bound for Argentina. Vatican assistance came via the *Pontificia Commissione di Assistenza* (PCA), a department set up by Pope Pius XII to help refugees. On application, in any name but claiming statelessness, a letter of recommendation would be supplied with a few lines confirming the new identity, together with the letterhead and the signature of the PCA. This was enough to guarantee the supply of a passport from the International Red Cross, enough in turn to obtain visas and travel documents for any intended destinations.

Others travelled south, making for the Italian capital, usually staying in monasteries along what became known as the Roman Way. There were two key ratlines in operation in Rome. One was organized by the Austrian bishop Alois Hudal, rector of the German-speaking national church in Rome, Santa Maria dell'Anima. A publicly acclaimed supporter of Hitler, his dream, according to the German theologian Maximilian Liebmann, was to be a bridge-builder between the Nazis and the Catholic Church. Although Hudal was operating independently of the Vatican by 1945, he continued to live in the Anima College. Hudal did much to give the Catholic Church its reputation as an escape route for Nazis. Although stories that he had a gold membership card for the Nazi Party are probably untrue, he was sympathetic to National Socialist beliefs – though not to the extent of believing in the Führer as God. His hatred of communism and his intense nationalism drove him to help fleeing Nazis, enabling hundreds of war criminals and others to escape to Argentina, North Africa and the Middle East.

The other ratline was operated by Krunoslav Draganović, a former member of the fascist Ustaše organization and a high-ranking Catholic bishop posted to the Italian capital in 1943. Armed with inner circle connections at the Vatican, he organized his smuggling network at the church of San Girolamo (St Jerome), which covered Italy, Austria and Germany. During the war, the Independent State of Croatia had operated as a puppet state of Nazi Germany. It was a one-party state, governed by the Ustaše leader Ante Pavelić. One of the most lethal regimes of the 20th century, the regime targeted, among other minorities, Serbs, Jews and Gypsies in a large-scale campaign of genocide. Draganović, who supported Pavelić's racial programme, served as chaplain at Jasenovac concentration camp, where it is estimated that 750,000 people died horrific deaths at the hands of brutal Ustaše thugs.

Draganović ran an efficient ratline route with the help of several other senior Catholic prelates in Rome, Genoa and Vienna who had previously served in the Ustaše and were themselves war criminals. At the end of the war, Pavelić and some of his most loyal and brutal mass murderers made their way to Austria in fear of reprisals. They were housed in a monastery in Salzburg and supplied with Red Cross documents to permit travel along the ratline to Rome by Father Vilim Cecelja. In Rome, they lived in church property, often travelling around the city in Vatican vehicles with diplomatic plates, which could therefore not be stopped. When his presence in the city was discovered by US intelligence, Pavelić was allowed to leave for South America to avoid Vatican embarrassment. He used money stolen from victims of extermination and given to him by Father Dominic Mandić from San Girolamo's coffers, and tickets provided by Monsignor Karlo Petranović, Draganović's agent in Genoa. Travelling under the name Pablo Aranyos, Pavelić left Italy on 13 September 1947, arriving in Buenos

Aires on 6 November aboard the Italian ship SS *Sestriera*. His arrival completed the transfer of almost his entire government to Argentina (see Chapter 7).

ARGENTINA AND ELSEWHERE

Files recently discovered in Argentina reveal a list of 12,000 former Nazis living there in the 1930s. This link was not new, as German influence was well established across the whole of South America, and Argentina in particular, by the turn of the 20th century. The considerable influx of immigrants not only from Germany, but also Italy and Spain, ensured Argentina retained its long-held close ties with all three European countries. During World War II, and certainly with the rise of the Nazis, the link was mutually nurtured. Germany promised Argentina trade deals and economic relations at the conclusion of the war, in return for its support.

In 1946, Juan Domingo Perón became president of Argentina. A populist who was elected on a ticket supporting the poor and the working class, he had served in Mussolini's Italian fascist army in the 1930s and was openly supportive of Hitler. As president, he made it clear that he would welcome any former Nazis who wanted to come and live in Argentina. Although it was not confirmed until the late 1970s, he was also personally active in overseeing the safe passage of hundreds or even thousands of SS members in the years after the war. Many took the ratlines through Italy and Spain, using looted Jewish funds, art and jewels to buy their way to freedom, paying whoever they could trust to help their safe passage.

For Argentina, the benefits were big. Many Nazis arrived with money, skills and experience. Money was invested in industries and factories, skills were utilized by German-owned companies, and Perón himself was interested in taking on experienced military leaders and aircraft designers of the Third Reich who wanted to make his home their home. Once on Argentinian soil, the Patagonian town of Bariloche was an attractive destination for these desperate men. In a beautiful Alpine lakeland setting near the Chilean border, it was far from prying eyes and had been home to a German community for over a hundred years.

Argentina was not the only South American country to offer shelter to Nazi fugitives. Peru, Chile, Paraguay and Brazil also proved to be safe havens for those fleeing Allied justice, though mostly after Perón was ousted from power in 1955. An anti-Perónist wave spread across the country following his defeat, and many former Nazis feared they would be hunted down and shipped back to Europe to face trial. Most of them dispersed to neighbouring countries, keeping a low profile with the help of adopted aliases. Some were more successful at avoiding detection than others (see Chapter 10).

That this mass escape happened, often in plain sight of the Allied authorities in Europe, points to the fact that the separate interests of the parties involved made for a fortuitous convergence. For different reasons, both the Allies and Argentina felt it was in their best interests to let these war criminals escape. Taking one of these routes allowed some of the Nazi regime's most notorious killers to escape justice, including: Adolf Eichmann, one of the most hunted fugitives in history; Josef Mengele, the notorious and sadistic 'doctor of Auschwitz'; Walter Rauff, inventor of the mobile gas chambers; Gerhard Bohne, who worked on the Aktion T4 euthanasia programme; Franz Stangl, commandant of the Sobibor and Treblinka death camps in Poland; Josef Schwammberger, the sadistic labour camp commander; Erich Priebke, the SS commander who helped organize the Ardeatine Caves massacre of 335 Italian partisans in Rome; and the notorious Klaus Barbie, better known as the 'Butcher of Lyon'. For the Allies, the Nazis were losing their sheen: it was expensive to pursue them, the need for revenge was weakening, and there was another enemy – the communists.

YOU SCRATCH MY BACK

In the final few weeks of the war, as the first Nazis gathered in South Tyrol to plan their escape through the mountains to northern Italy, Allen Dulles, representative of the Office of Strategic Services (OSS, forerunner of the CIA) in Switzerland, was negotiating the surrender of German forces in that theatre with SS general Karl Wolff. With the fighting ending here earlier than in northern Europe, Dulles was among the first to open channels of communication with high-ranking SS officers. Dulles and his brother, John Foster – Secretary of State to President Dwight D. Eisenhower – were already enthusiastic supporters of the rehabilitation of Germany as an ally against the rising tide of Soviet communism. This initial connection was to prove useful to both sides.

The Allies were, of course, aware of the existence of the ratlines. At first, theirs was a policy of observation, enabling them to track the movements of former Nazis and collaborators, but all that changed in September 1945 when Major General Reinhard Gehlen arrived in Washington DC, having surrendered to US forces in Bavaria. A leading Wehrmacht intelligence officer, and a member of The Odessa (see page 148), an organization of former SS members who had already established their own ratline, Gehlen was the leading expert on the Red Army and their battlefield tactics. He had also built up a huge mass of

Nazi criminal Erich Priebke on trial in Rome in 1996 for the Ardeatine Caves massacre in Rome.

intelligence files on eastern Europe and the Soviet Union in particular, which contained vital information for the Americans in their fight against the 'new' communist threat.

The result of his trip was the establishment of a US-German intelligence network specifically to spy on the Soviet Union. In July 1946, the Gehlen Org, as it was called, began its work, employing agents throughout the Soviet Bloc to provide information for the CIA – for example, on developments inside Warsaw Pact nations, eavesdropping activities and monitoring the size of the Russian missile fleet. Among its employees were former members of the Wehrmacht, the SS and the Gestapo, including Alois Brunner, Adolf Eichmann's assistant, SS Major Emil Augsburg, mass murderer of Polish Jews and other 'undesirables', Frank Six, who oversaw the killings of hundreds of Jews in the Smolensk ghetto, and Klaus Barbie.

Barbie, a notorious ex-Gestapo chief who was responsible for the murder of thousands of French Jews and members of the resistance, represented a new aspect of the use of the ratlines. According to now declassified US Army intelligence reports, in 1950 US forces began using Draganović's network to evacuate its own 'visitors', as they were called. Barbie was 'recruited' for his anti-communist stance and his knowledge of British interrogation techniques and French intelligence activities. This had been done in the full knowledge that Barbie was wanted by the French government to face criminal charges.

Just like Perón in Argentina, the US was keen not to miss out on potential assets among the Nazi technicians, scientists and former military strategists fleeing Germany. This tactic was to reach its apex with the covert operations Bloodstone and Paperclip, both part of the US Cold War campaign. The first of these was to recruit former Nazis and collaborators for use as intelligence and covert operation experts to perform 'propaganda, economic warfare, sabotage, anti-sabotage, demolition and evacuation measures' against the Soviet state, and offer assistance to any resistance movements, anti-communist elements, guerrillas and refugee liberation groups in [communist] threatened countries of the free world. Operation Paperclip saw more than 1,600 German scientists, engineers and technicians – many of them former members of the Nazi Party – taken to the US between 1945 and 1959 to give it an advantage over the Soviets in the Cold War and the space race (see Chapter 9).

OTHER RATLINES, OTHER ORGANIZATIONS

There were many routes out of Germany, in all directions. As a result of demand, other ratlines developed, supported by other countries, Nazi support groups, right-wing political groups, former soldiers, ship-owners and shady businessmen keen to make some money. It was a confusing picture and, although there were risks attached, the potential rewards were tempting.

Connections between Switzerland and Germany were obvious, in terms of geography, border controls, banking and trade. Its 'non-involvement' policy, officially proclaimed in 1815, was severely tested during World War II, and historians still argue about it. In reality, by 1940 Switzerland was completely surrounded by Axis powers and only avoided invasion by the Nazis because they were preoccupied elsewhere and because the Swiss banks proved a useful repository for the Nazis' ill-gotten gains. But there was more. The Swiss imposed strict laws to regulate the influx of Jewish refugees, in many cases denying entry completely and otherwise taxing the local Jewish community for any refugees allowed in. Worse still were the accusations that the Swiss banks hid large amounts of gold collected from Holocaust victims sent to the death camps, and that they also gave the Nazis assistance in terms of money laundering. Senior Swiss officials, such as the president of the International Committee of the Red Cross Carl Jacob Burckhardt and police chief Heinrich Rothmund – both seriously anti-communist – were also suspected of allowing Nazis to pass freely across their borders and into Italy. Together with Argentine-born former SS member Carlos Fuldner, who had contacts with Perón's chief of intelligence, Rothmund and others are said to have facilitated the escape of many war criminals to Buenos Aires.

While Switzerland was neutral, Sweden declared itself 'non-belligerent' in 1939 and, for the most part, was able to maintain this policy throughout the war, offering concessions to both Nazi Germany and the Allies, retaining trade links and even offering help to Finland when it was attacked by the Red Army in 1939. In fact, some Swedes fought for Germany and some for the Allies; it was a personal choice rather than Swedish government policy. However, Sweden has been home to far-right movements since the early years of the 20th century, and in 1945, Per Engdahl, the leader of the Swedish fascist movement, organized an escape route though his network, later known as the Malmö Movement. It smuggled Nazis through northern Germany and Denmark to his hometown of Malmö. From there, they were moved to various places in southern Sweden, and then sent by ship from Gothenburg to South America.

Some returned to Germany, because US authorities had begun releasing former members of the SS due to the expense of keeping them locked up. In this way, Engdahl claimed to have 'saved' about 4,000 Nazis.

The name Odessa (*Organisation Der Ehemaligen SS-Angehörigen* – Organization of Former Members of the SS) has passed into popular consciousness mainly due to Frederick Forsyth's book *The Odessa File* (published in 1972) and the subsequent film, which relates the story of how former SS officers got together after the war to help high-ranking Nazis escape from Germany, with the aim of rebuilding their organization and setting up a Fourth Reich. While admitting that there were some genuine historical facts in the novel, many historians were sceptical about the existence of such an organization. However, Holocaust survivor and Nazi hunter Simon Wiesenthal was convinced of its existence from the moment he heard about it during the course of the Nuremberg trials.

He believed that a network was established as early as 1944 at a secret meeting of industrialists, including steel magnate Fritz Thyssen, in Strasbourg. Delegates agreed that an escape route was needed quickly, as the likelihood of German defeat and the fear of subsequent reprisals made it paramount. Those involved in the early stages of the organization included: Charles Lesca (see page 136); Otto Abetz, the German ambassador to Paris; and Argentinian president Juan Domingo Perón, who set up a new government department for the purpose.

It is rumoured that the most famous 'members' of Odessa were Erich Priebke, Josef Mengele and Adolf Eichmann, although thousands of Nazis are said to have been helped by this secret network. How organized it was in reality has never fully come to light, and it is most likely that the routes it used came together in a haphazard fashion as the last option for a group of frightened and desperate fugitives running for their lives. Another organization, said by some to be a branch of Odessa, was *Die Spinne* (The Spider). Formed in Madrid in

1945 by Otto Skorzeny (see Chapter 8) – Hitler's commando chief – and intelligence chief Reinhard Gehlen (see page 143), the organization is said to have helped 600 Nazis, including Mengele, escape to South America and the Middle East.

There was also help available for those Nazis who had not escaped. *Stille Hilfe* (Silent Assistance) was set up in 1951 to help former SS members who had been arrested, condemned or were otherwise at risk. It had operated a ratline since 1946, but reorganized itself as a non-profit association in search of funds from the Catholic Church, the aristocracy and the upper middle-class conservatives. Its first president was Helene Elisabeth, Princess von Isenburg, chosen for her wide network of contacts. Its early concerns centred around those on trial at Nuremberg, organizing legal assistance, trying to influence public opinion against any death sentences and offering help to those who were sentenced to hang.

As well as Princess von Isenburg, prominent members of *Stille Hilfe* included Gudrun Burwitz, daughter of Heinrich Himmler, and Johannes Neuhäusler, a high-ranking church representative who had been imprisoned by the Gestapo and sent to Dachau. Neuhäusler said he wanted to 'repay the bad with the good', an opinion that featured widely in new post-war West Germany. Although it is still in existence, *Stille Hilfe* has had its charitable status rescinded, and in recent years has drawn criticism for neo-Nazi connections.

A similar veterans association, *Hilfsgemeinschaft auf Gegenseitigkeit der Angehörigen der ehemaligen Waffen-SS* (mutual aid association of former Waffen-SS members), was a lobby group and a denialist organization founded by former high-ranking Waffen-SS officers in West Germany in 1951. Its objective was to achieve legal, economic and historical rehabilitation of the Waffen-SS. Initially successful in its argument that Waffen-SS soldiers had been treated worse than others in their POW camps, its reputation suffered over the years due to the 'consistently racist, anti-Semitic and anti-democratic' opinions expressed by various members. As the German public's awareness of SS atrocities grew during the 1970s and 1980s, the idea that the Waffen-SS had not been directly involved in the killings of prisoners of war or other Nazi atrocities was completely discredited. The group was finally disbanded in 1992.

While most Nazi support groups were based in Germany, one – *Kameradenwerk* (comrades' work) – was set up in Argentina by former ground-attack pilot Hans-Ulrich Rudel, the most decorated German serviceman of World War II. Having surrendered to US forces in 1945, Rudel made his way via the ratline to Rome and on to Buenos Aires in 1948. A committed and unrepentant National Socialist, he founded his relief organization to help Nazis escape Germany and get to South America or the Middle East in safety, as well as sending food parcels and helping with legal fees for Nazi criminals imprisoned in Europe, such as Rudolf Hess and Karl Dönitz. He became friends with Juan Perón, through whom he secured lucrative contracts with the Brazilian military and the Bolivian regime, with Augusto Pinochet in Chile, and Alfredo Stroessner in Paraguay. He returned to Germany in 1953 to enter politics as a member of the neo-Nazi German Reich Party (DRP), but was not elected to the Bundestag in the federal election that year. He died in 1982.

While the number of Nazis who escaped prosecution for war crimes by leaving Germany along the ratlines is impossible to estimate, there is evidence of escape routes leading to

Argentina, Paraguay, Ecuador, Colombia, Chile, Peru, Brazil, Bolivia and Uruguay in South America; Mexico and Guatemala in Central America; the US; Canada; Spain, Portugal, Austria, Switzerland and Ireland in Europe; Algeria, Egypt and Tunisia in North Africa; Saudi Arabia, Syria and Iran in the Middle East; and Afghanistan and Pakistan in Asia. All of these ratlines had their strings pulled by the ratmasters.

THE RATMASTERS

IN THE latter years of the 1940s, the pre-war tourists had only just begun to return to the exhausted city of Rome. In the magnificent Piazza Navona, there were a few signs of returning life. The odd black sedan or occasional US army jeep trundled around the cobbled street that still traced out the ancient perimeter of the Emperor Domitian's stadium. Most days, there were a few sightseers, usually small groups of Allied servicemen, or sailors on a few days' leave from the British and American fleets moored off Naples. As ever, the *maneggioni*, or spivs, who plied their trade on the streets of post-war Rome, held out stolen watches and similar contraband for these few uniformed tourists. A handful of country women had returned to the square, sitting beneath Bernini's monumental fountains, peddling their baskets of fruit and flowers. The famous Bar Tre Scalini had just opened on the western side of the 'square'. And as always in the Eternal City, priests in long black cassocks scuttled to and from the many churches in this particular district of Rome.

In 1946, the careful listener in Piazza Navona and its surrounding narrow, shadowed alleyways would have often heard the distinct tones of German speech, especially when groups of younger priests passed by. Only a few steps away from the western side of the piazza stood the historic hub of German life in Rome, the church of Santa Maria dell'Anima, Our Lady of the Soul. A small wooden sign by the central door of the Anima's restrained façade displayed the legend: 'Here God hears prayers in the German tongue.' The church had long been the spiritual home of the city's German and Austrian congregation. The complex of austere buildings directly behind it formed part of the Teutonic Papal College, where Catholic novices from the Germanic north came to pursue their vocation. In the decade after the war, however, there was a very noticeable rise in the number of German voices heard in and around the Anima; they mostly belonged to men who had no intention of taking the cloth, but who certainly needed the help of the Church.

THE BROWNSHIRT BISHOP

Since 1923, the rector of the seminary within the Anima compound had been the Austrian cleric and academic Alois Hudal, a small, good-natured man who was to become one of the most controversial Roman Catholic priests of the 20th century. Hudal had enjoyed a career as a researcher, thinker and teacher at his home university of Graz in Styria, and had made a favourable public impression during his service as a military padre in World War I. Once posted to Rome, he also proved to be an effective pastor to the city's Austro-Germanic congregation and a reliable source of sound advice when the Vatican turned its attention to issues affecting Catholic Austria. His talents were rewarded in 1933 when he was elevated to the rank of bishop. After this highpoint, his career in the Church stalled as his increasingly forthright political views diverged from the official neutrality of the Church during the papacy

Austrian bishop Alois Hudal was head of the Austrian-German congregation of Santa Maria dell'Anima in Rome, and an admirer of Hitler. He helped to establish the ratlines for Nazi fugitives.

of Pius XI. Hudal's early writings on ecclesiastical and biblical matters had marked him out as a moderate if conservative man, and therefore 'a safe pair of hands'. After Hitler took power in Germany, however, Hudal's work took a more pressing political direction, reflecting a change in the international climate across Europe after 1933.

Like many Catholic leaders of his generation, Hudal feared that the eternal message of Christianity was facing a deadly onslaught from the secular attitudes promoted in Western democracies and by Soviet Russia. And like many conservative Austrians, he drew links between the rise of liberalism, socialism and Marxism, and he suspected the influence of international Jewry behind these movements. He resented the increasing predominance of 'Jewish-Marxist' ideas in the universities, and he especially feared the godless Bolsheviks and their international communist movement that seemed to be spreading its tentacles around the globe. Hudal was inevitably attracted to the strands in National Socialist propaganda that portrayed the New Germany as a military and moral bulwark against the Red Menace in the East. In the middle years of the decade, Hudal increasingly felt that the Catholic Church needed to find a way of working with the new German regime that seemed to him to represent 'the hope for the future'.

In 1937, Hudal published *Foundations of National Socialism*, a book that attempted to find common ground between Catholicism and Nazism. Failing to understand the true ruthlessness of the Nazi movement, he naively believed that the Catholic Church could work with Hitler and his government, and so continue to be responsible for the moral education of Germany's young. In return, the Church would lend its support to the Party in its struggle against international communism. Hudal hoped that the influence of the Church would 'Christianize' the brutal moral tone of the Nazis. In the copy of his book that he personally sent to the Führer, Hudal compared Hitler to the great Wagnerian hero Siegfried. Hitler was flattered, expressed some interest in Hudal's ideas and permitted the printing of a very limited edition of the book for the perusal of party intellectuals such as Alfred Rosenberg. The Nazi leadership, however, had its own plans for educating the young of the Third Reich, which were far removed from Hudal's dream of a vigorous but virtuous Christian National Socialism.

The publication of his book, plus some intemperate public comments that Hudal made, which were anti-Semitic and overtly pro-German, blocked any further advancement within the Church. He had also gone to press without seeking the official permission from the Church authorities in Rome. His positive view of the German annexation of Austria in 1938 embarrassed the papacy at a difficult time, when it was desperately trying to maintain the semblance of neutrality and detachment from political events in Europe. Hudal's evident sympathy for aspects of Nazism won him the dubious nickname of the Brown or Brownshirt Bishop. He was no longer welcome at senior meetings in the Vatican, effectively banished by the Church establishment and increasingly isolated within his seminary. In fact, this enforced distance from the machinery of Church government across the river Tiber was to prove useful in his activities during and after the war.

SANCTUARY

Like many Catholic institutions across Europe throughout the war, Hudal's walled enclave offered shelter to desperate men and women on the run: displaced refugees, hunted members of the Resistance and even a few Allied servicemen who had escaped from POW camps. Hudal even wrote in 1943 to General Stahel, the German military commander in the city, asking him to suspend the terror activities against the Jews in Rome, and won some temporary relief for that ancient community. But after the fall of the Third Reich, the Brown Bishop turned his church and its seminary into a shelter for the hundreds of German refugees who were making their way along the main ratline that led south through the Alpine passes deep into Italy. Hudal knew that many of these refugees were wanted war criminals, but took the view that he was helping desperate men who were unfortunate souls and 'victims of history'. In a letter to General Perón of Argentina, he asked: 'When in human history was military service ever a moral crime, barring the door to a peaceful and honest future?' Ignoring the growing evidence of the Holocaust and the other savage war crimes committed across Europe during the age of Hitler, Bishop Hudal justified his actions by claiming that he was only helping men who had sacrificed their all in the fight against insidious Bolshevism.

The rambling complex of the Anima was well placed to serve as a refuge. It was situated right in the heart of civic Rome and was more than a kilometre outside the medieval walls of the Vatican. Yet it was legally considered to belong to the old Church State, and therefore not part of Italy. Thanks to an agreement between Mussolini and the papacy in 1929, the Anima enjoyed extra-territorial diplomatic privileges. The power of Italian law and the Italian police stopped at its gates. It was a perfect sanctuary for refugees, including war criminals, who could wait safely behind its doors for the best moment to set out on the next leg of their voyage to a new life far from Allied justice.

BISHOP HUDAL'S HELPERS

In addition to a safe address in Rome, Hudal could also provide support for Nazis needing a new identity and practical help in order to escape. As one of the most prominent German-speaking prelates in Rome, he knew the wealthy Austrian and German families still resident in Rome. He also knew which ones could be persuaded to help their countrymen in distress with some cash and other material supplies. In 1944, Hudal came in from the Vatican cold when he was appointed to oversee the *Assistenza Austriaca*, the Vatican's diplomatic section charged with assisting Austrian refugees. This position gave him the right to visit prisoner-of-war camps across central Italy, where many of his compatriots had ended up. He later remembered that this allowed him 'to visit and comfort many victims in their prisons and aid their escape with fresh papers'.

Once safely in the Anima, fugitive Nazis received a new identity card issued by Hudal's bureau, often expertly forged by a former SS captain, Reinhard Kopps, who had an office in the seminary. With this first official Vatican card, it was easier for the holder to get the subsequent documents that would cement their new name deeper in the paperwork. The next step for the ratliner was usually to make their way to Genoa where the Franciscan Father Dömöter maintained a safe house in one of the narrow, cobbled alleyways close to the harbour quays. Kopps and Dömöter were both skilled at inventing plausible back-stories for fugitives and offering advice on how to negotiate escape routes. Hudal also had links to friendly diplomats in key embassies in Rome. They could help to arrange travel documents and tickets on ships bound for South America or the Middle East. He had friends in the church hierarchy in Genoa, who ministered to the sympathetic businessmen running the shipping lines out of that port. The escapee with assets could always buy his own ticket, but many had to be helped from Hudal's limited funds. When those ran out, the penniless often had to wait in Dömöter's shelter until a last-minute message came from a ship to say that legitimate passengers had failed to turn up and an empty berth had suddenly become available. Hudal also had useful allies at the other end of the transatlantic ratline, such as Antonio Caggiano, bishop of the Argentinian port of Rosario. Caggiano ran his own ratline helping French collaborators to avoid 'harsh measures and private vengeance', and he could always be relied on to help clandestine Nazi travellers with the next stage of their journey. Hudal had other contacts among the highest levels of Argentinian society. It was no surprise in 1947 when he was invited to a reception organized by the city authorities at the Rome Golf Club on the Via Appia for their glamorous guest, Eva Perón.

One of Hudal's contacts, the Swiss diplomat and history professor Carl Jacob Burckhardt, was immensely useful in helping dubious refugees get out of Europe. Steeped in German culture and history, Burckhardt served as the League of Nation's high commissioner in Danzig during its last years as a free city in the late 1930s. In the course of his duties, he met Hitler and many of his senior ministers as they planned to take the city back under German control. Burckhardt carried out his duties for the League and for Danzig in a conscientious and well-balanced manner. Yet he understood the ethnic and historic urges that fuelled the Nazi desire to right what they saw as one of the wrongs inflicted upon Germany by the 1919 peace settlement. After the war, Burckhardt served as president of the International Committee of the Red Cross from 1945 to 1948. He passionately believed that the ICRC should remain above the prevailing mood of punitive vengeance that he feared would make it difficult for a new peaceful Europe to emerge from the rubble. As a result, the ICRC adopted a strict neutrality in its policies and actions when dealing with migrants and refugees. It was a stance that many war criminals were able to exploit. Possession of a Vatican identity card and a letter of recommendation signed by Bishop Hudal was never questioned by the ICRC officials responsible for issuing valuable Red Cross passports.

HUDAL'S TOP RATS

The number of German fugitives who used Hudal's ratline in the late 1940s will never be known with certainty. A letter survives from Hudal to President Perón dated August 1948, asking for 5,000 blank Argentinian visas for 'anti-communist warriors', which suggests that the Brown Bishop was running a full-scale operation. Not all of the Germans who passed through the Anima were war criminals, but the list of known 'Hudal rats' contains many exceptionally guilty men who were deeply involved in the running of the Nazi extermination machinery.

Originally a naval officer, by the late 1930s Walter Rauff was a senior officer in the SS, trusted by Himmler and a good friend of Reinhard Heydrich, another of the main architects of the Holocaust. Rauff's main claim to infamy was his development of the mobile gas chamber in 1941–42. He had witnessed the mass shootings of 'undesirables' such as Jews and Roma in eastern Europe and had discussed the problems of this method of extermination with fellow SS officers. They agreed that shooting was a slow and inefficient procedure, and that the men in the murder detachments were often affected by the 'burden' of carrying out their orders. Rauff therefore developed the mobile gas chamber in an attempt to industrialize and dehumanize mass murder. Unwanted victims in a locked van were killed by the carbon monoxide issuing from the vehicle's diverted exhaust. Up to sixty souls would die an unseen death as they were being driven to their pre-dug graves. In late 1942, Rauff played a major part in the destruction of the Jewish community in Vichy-run Tunisia, and the confiscation of their wealth. The following year he enhanced his reputation for ruthlessness when he commanded all SS, SD and Gestapo activities in north-west Italy. With the war clearly turning against the Axis powers by late 1943, he seems to have made contact with Bishop Hudal to discuss ways of dealing with the human consequences of German defeat. After only just escaping an angry mob in liberated Milan and then eluding the partisans, Rauff ended up in a British POW camp in Rimini, where his true identity went undetected. Thanks to Hudal, he was soon free and hiding in various convents and monasteries en route for Rome. In late 1944, he certainly met the bishop when he began an 18-month spell within the walls of the Anima seminary, keeping a low profile. And it was the resources of the Anima ratline that helped him move on to Syria, Ecuador and finally Chile.

Gustav Wagner and Franz Stangl had similar careers after 1939. Both were ambitious SS officers who learned their skills in mass murder working on the Aktion T4 Euthanasia programme. Both graduated to posts at the concentration camp at Sobibor, a village in the heart of pre-war Poland, and both held positions of responsibility there. Stangl was the first commander at Sobibor from late April to August 1942. He was an efficient administrator who took a cold, detached view of his job. In Stangl's four short months in charge at the camp, approximately 100,000 units of 'cargo', as he preferred to call the inmates, were murdered. His expertise and dedication were appreciated by Himmler, and he was soon transferred to sort out some irritating efficiency problems at Treblinka. Stangl was known as the 'White Death' on account of his sparkling white uniform, but he kept himself aloof from the daily running of the camp and especially distant from its Jewish prisoners. Killing the required daily quotas was a necessary element of his professional duties, but he does not seem to have indulged in any individual acts of brutality. His deputy Gustav Wagner was much more involved at the business end of extermination. Known as the 'Beast of Sobibor', Wagner was the principal selection officer who scanned new arrivals and sealed their fate within seconds. After the war, witnesses testified that Wagner had shot and killed numerous individuals seemingly on a whim, when simply displeased by some aspect of his victim's appearance or behaviour. Witnesses also noted the immense pleasure that he received from these random acts of terror. He had been heard to express disappointment and frustration with the overall tally of the Sobibor dead whenever it lagged behind the much more impressive extermination results at Treblinka and Belzec. After the war, both Wagner and Stangl were helped by Hudal: Wagner stayed at the Anima for more than eight months. By 1950, he was living in Brazil under the name of Günther Mendel. After a spell in Syria, Stangl also ended up in Brazil, where he eventually worked for Volkswagen. Neither man ever expressed any regret for their wartime actions.

Other notable Hudal rats included Erich Priebke, one of the SS officers responsible for the reprisal killing of 335 Italian citizens at the Ardeatine Caves just outside Rome. After lying low in monasteries at Sterzing or Vipiteno in the South Tyrol for three years, a package for Priebke arrived from Rome containing papers with his new identity as Otto Pope, and a

Franz Stangl was an Austrian police officer who joined the SS and worked for the Nazis' T4 euthanasia programme, then in concentration camps. He described Jewish victims of the Nazis as 'cargo'.

ticket for Argentina. The Nazi SS lawyer Eduard Roschmann had been in charge of controlling the Jewish ghetto in Riga. Although Roschmann does not seem to have committed murder himself, he was ultimately responsible for the many individual killings of Jews in the city during his period of office. He spent much of the first three years after the war in Allied custody, but eventually escaped and made his way to Genoa, then Argentina, thanks to an International Red Cross passport sourced by the Brown Bishop. The Luftwaffe hero Hans-Ulrich Rudel was not wanted for specific war crimes, but he was a living symbol of the Third Reich as he was said to be the most highly decorated German combatant in World War II. His exploits on the Eastern Front were endlessly relayed to the German public on cinema newsreels, and some of his many honours were presented by the Führer himself. Rudel lost his right leg as a result of enemy action in February 1945, but he continued to fly and fight until the very end of the war. He even managed to get into Berlin to meet with Hitler in the *Führerbunker* 11 days before Hitler's suicide. Rudel managed to go west and surrender himself to the Americans and therefore escape Russian justice. In 1948, he slipped through South Tyrol and took advantage of Hudal's hospitality in central Rome while waiting for a fresh Red Cross passport and a flight to Buenos Aires.

Not all refugees managed to complete the journey from defeated Germany to freedom elsewhere, despite help from the Anima. Otto Wächter had successfully hidden in the West Tyrol mountains throughout the first four post-war years, sustained by secret food drops organized by his family. He finally set off for Rome in 1949. As governor of Krakow and then of the province of Galicia during the war, Wächter had a great deal of blood on his hands, much of it Jewish. Nevertheless, Hudal welcomed him and found secret lodgings for him in a small religious foundation on the outskirts of Rome while his papers and transit plans were organized. By 3 July, Wächter had been moved to the Anima, where he was known to enjoy a daily swim in the nearby Tiber. Eleven days later he was dead from kidney failure and a high fever. It was assumed that he had fallen victim to the notorious pollution in the river and, of course, it was said that he had never been a well man. Others heard rumours that the dead man's tongue was blue, a sure sign that he had been poisoned. Was his death an accident, had he taken his own life to evade justice, or had he been despatched by his enemies? Whatever the cause of his death, Bishop Hudal did his priestly duty by this servant of National Socialism, staying at his bedside throughout his final days and administering the last rites.

In his own words, Hudal spent the next three years 'comforting victims in their prisons and helping them escape from their tormentors'. He felt no remorse at helping wanted war criminals, and he continued to defend his actions in speeches and in his writing until his death in 1962. He resigned from his post of rector at the Anima in 1952, jumping before he was pushed out by the Vatican, which was increasingly embarrassed by the openness of his activities. In his bitter memoirs, he lashed out at Pope Pius XII and his officials in the Vatican who failed to help 'men who had sacrificed everything to save Europe from Bolshevism'. In fact, recent scholars have found that in its own mysterious way, the Catholic Church did channel some funds designated for humanitarian aid towards Hudal's ratline operation, if not in the amounts that the bishop hoped for. Other documents suggest that Pius had long been very well aware of what was going on in the Anima and 'allowed himself to overlook it'.

THE REFUGE OF ST JEROME

From its beginnings, the Roman church of San Girolamo (St Jerome) was a place of refuge. When the Ottoman Turks captured the great city of Constantinople in 1453, thousands of frightened Christians fled from the Balkans and headed westwards. Many made their way to Rome. That same year, Pope Nicholas V gifted a stretch of neglected ground and some dilapidated church buildings to a small brotherhood of Balkan priests who were trying to arrange shelter for the large number of their compatriots flooding into the city. Over time, this largely Croat community built a new church to their national saint, Jerome of Dalmatia, on a site that lies a short walk north of the Ponte Sant'Angelo, close to the Ripetta steps where the Tiber fishermen traditionally landed their catches. A monastery, a hospital and a seminary for Croatian Catholic novices followed. In 1945 and 1946, a group of keen young men could be seen maintaining a 24-hour vigil at the gates of this high-walled complex of religious buildings. However, their casual clothing, darkened glasses, rough language and fondness for cigarettes all suggested that they were not candidates for the priesthood. The interested passer-by could also see that the young men were nervous and frequently took handguns out from within their jackets to check and clean them, or perhaps simply to bolster their confidence. Visitors to the complex were rigorously questioned and vigorously frisked. All documents were checked and then scrutinized again. British and American Intelligence learned that these guards were only the first line of security at the Croatian complex. All the main doors within the monastery and college were kept locked, bolted and guarded by men who were even more heavily armed. These included uniformed troops who exchanged the distinctive salute of the Croatian fascistic movement, the Ustaše.

The word on the streets of Rome was that the Girolamo had been turned into a fortress in order to protect vast fortunes carried there following the collapse of the Nazi puppet state of Croatia. Within its brick walls, there were said to be untold millions of dollars in gold and other kinds of loot sequestered, extorted and stolen by the Nazis and their Ustaše allies, not just from Yugoslavia but from all over south-eastern Europe. According to other rumours, more than 20 million Swiss Francs extorted from Croatian Jews had already been transferred from a bank in the city to a senior Croatian cleric. Allied intelligence reports speculated that when Ante Pavelić, the Poglavnik or Great Leader of Croatia, attempted to flee from justice in May 1945, he tried to carry $80 million in gold coins with him. The criminal Ustaše government certainly amassed huge fortunes during its four years of absolute power, particularly from its Jewish victims. Much of these monies was squirreled away and eventually laundered, but even in the pre-digital age there were more convenient methods of moving money than transporting bulky hard cash all the way from Croatia to Rome. The guards at the gates of St Jerome were really there to protect the seven or more Croatian government ministers hiding inside its walls. They were desperate men who were anxiously waiting to be spirited away to safer destinations far from Allied prosecutors and from the vengeance of fellow Yugoslavs seeking revenge for the attempted annihilation of their communities during the four years of Ustaše terror.

THE BALKAN RATMASTER

The mastermind in charge of helping these Croatian runaways was a compatriot and a political sympathizer. Despite his clerical garb, he was also almost certainly a war criminal himself. Monsignor Krunoslav Draganović was a tall, busy man who barely broke step as he walked unhindered past the guards protecting the Croatian compound. Like Hudal, he was an ardent anti-communist, but he had played a far more active part in the war than his Austrian counterpart. A convinced believer in the 'Germanic' superiority of the Croats over their Slavic neighbours, he was a member of the Ustaše movement. He served the puppet state as a member of its Board of Colonization. Its main function was to promote cultural uniformity by forcing Orthodox Serbs to convert to Catholicism and to deal with those who refused. The Board was not squeamish in carrying out its remit. Witnesses later claimed that Draganović had been present at a number of atrocities carried out to crush resistance in Serb towns and villages. For a time, he was chaplain at the Jasenovac concentration camp, where almost 100,000 men, women and children were slaughtered. Given the public nature of many of these deaths, he must have been fully aware of the horrors committed there. Like Hudal, after the war he was given permission to visit Balkan prisoners held in Allied custody in Italy; it was noted that he only helped Croatians and ignored Serbian and Bosnian inmates. He also had sympathetic contacts within the Vatican – people quick to help fellow countrymen who had repented of their wartime crimes and now needed Christian help. The most important of these was the Franciscan priest Dominik Mandić, who was an administrator of his order's considerable financial assets. After 1945, Mandić became the chief source of support for Draganović's ratline, providing cash and fresh identity cards. Thanks to his connections with the Vatican Bank, Mandić also became an adept launderer of Ustaše loot that needed a new home elsewhere. It helped that the church of St Jerome had its 'own' powerful prelate at the

Vatican. In 1935, the Archbishop of Buenos Aires, Santiago Luis Copello, had become the first South American to be raised to the scarlet (appointed as cardinal), and St Jerome became his titular or personal church in the Eternal City. Cardinal Copello was deeply conservative and an avid supporter of General Perón's nationalist government – a useful man to know if you were operating an escape route to Argentina. Unsurprisingly, both Copello and Draganović met with Eva Perón in Rome during her 1947 Rainbow Tour of Europe.

A MINI MUSSOLINI

In the spring of 1946, Father Pedro Gonner, a priest of few words and those a fractured mixture of Spanish and Italian, arrived in Rome. Two years later, he appeared in Buenos Aires, but the name on his papers had changed to Señor Pablo Aranjos. His journey to South America had started in the picturesque village of St Gilgen (St Giles) in the Austrian Salzkammergut. There he had been known to the occupying American forces by his real name of Ante Pavelić, but they and the British agents in the district had failed to connect this tired refugee with the Poglavnik, the former Great Leader of the now collapsed fascist Croatia. Founder of the ultra-nationalist terrorist Ustaše in 1929 and a great admirer of Mussolini, Pavelić had spent time in Italy before. At first, the great dictator himself took little interest in his Balkan copycat. To appease the French, Mussolini had even detained him in an Italian prison from 1934 to 1936, while his part in the assassination of King Alexander of Yugoslavia in Marseille was investigated. Pavelić then spent much of the years 1937 to 1941 under relatively lax house arrest in Siena and Florence, 'detained' by the Italian authorities in case he might come in useful in the tangled mess that was the wartime

Balkans. Pavelić was little more than a useful tool in the larger game of European diplomacy in the 1930s. His big moment came in April 1941 when the Axis powers invaded and dissected Yugoslavia. With some reluctance, Hitler and Mussolini assented to the creation of a Croatian Ustaše government. Their reservations concerning Pavelić and his movement were well founded. The regime struggled to preserve its new state and lost ground to the ever-strengthening partisans: as one German commander noted, by late 1942 Pavelić was little more than mayor of 'Zagreb minus its suburbs'. The following year, Hitler's impatience with his incompetent puppet allies ran out; Croatian troops were merged into the German armed forces and required to swear loyalty directly to the Führer. The Pavelić administration had only one policy success: genocide. Although lacking the strength to cope with its military foes, it did manage to liquidate many of its internal enemies. Hated communities such as the Orthodox Serbs quickly lost their civil rights and were then persecuted by terror squads or shipped off to concentration camps; the Jewish and Roma communities in Croatia almost entirely disappeared. The total number of those massacred by the Pavelić regime in its short period of power has been estimated at upwards of 300,000.

As the war in Europe came to an end in the first week of May 1945, a pathetic exodus of demoralized Ustaše troops and civilians fled towards Austria in the hope of outrunning the Soviet and partisan forces close behind. Most of these fugitives were detained at the border by the British Army and returned to Yugoslavia in accordance with the protocols drawn up by the Allied leaders at the Yalta conference. They were marched back southwards to certain death. Pavelić had already made his own private plans for escape, however, and abandoned his doomed followers. He had little difficulty meeting up with his family, who had slipped out of the Balkans and into Austria six months earlier. In due course, Father Draganović was involved in arranging his travel and accommodation arrangements for his journey on to Rome. Once there, the Ustaše chief seems to have spent relatively little time at the Girolamo; by 1946, it was under constant surveillance by the official intelligence agencies operating in the city, as well as by various Balkan agents looking for a chance to strike at the most significant rat in Rome, a former Axis head of state. There were strong rumours that Pavelić was holed up in the exquisite palace of Castel Gandolfo, the papal summer residence overlooking Lake Albano in the hills 12 or so miles south of the city. This seemed probable: the palace was secure, exceptionally private and it enjoyed extra-territorial status, rendering it diplomatically impregnable. In fact, Draganović chose to hide his former boss somewhere much less obvious, in a dismal flat in a dark lane in Trastevere, at that time a decrepit and deprived district yet to flourish from the years of *la dolce vita* and international tourism. Pavelić spent more than two years there, transforming his appearance from the portly and pugnacious jack-booted fascist of his Zagreb days into the semblance of a much quieter chap altogether, a clerk or academic perhaps, with thick black circular glasses, an excessive moustache and bushy goatee beard. That disguise helped him to reach Buenos Aires in 1948, and it served him well for the following nine years there, until he was recognized by a Serbian anti-fascist. Pavelić was mortally wounded in a street attack in April 1957. Belated justice was finally delivered by two bullets that plugged into his back as he ran from his avenger.

A PERENNIAL SPY

By the late 1940s, Draganović had wound down much of his direct involvement in ratline activities. Most of the senior Ustaše who needed to escape Europe had done so. Time, events and the political climate moved on, yet Draganović was still involved in the same fight against communism that had first drawn him into Croatian politics. By 1947, however, he was gathering information about the Yugoslav communist regime of Marshal Tito, sending it not to his Poglavnik in Zagreb, but to the CIA. His single virtue for the Americans was his association with the Roman ratline that offered them a solution to relocation problems of people they wanted to 'rescue' from Nazi Germany. Special rats occasionally needed help, such as Klaus Barbie, the 'Butcher of Lyon', who had been recruited by the CIA in 1947 and who then received papers and support on his way to Bolivia in 1951, all expedited by Draganović.

In 1962, Draganović was regarded as no longer of value to US intelligence and was issued with a 'burn notice' dismissing him from his job. He returned to his native Bosnia in 1967 and avoided prosecution for his alleged war crimes in Yugoslavia, presumably in return for his 'support' of Tito's communist regime. He died in Sarajevo in June 1983, at the age of 79.

OTHER BOLTHOLES

In the immediate aftermath of the war, Alois Brunner considered himself a very lucky man. As a senior SS officer, he was deeply implicated in the Holocaust. He rightly guessed that the victorious Allies were looking for him and was well aware that he could expect little mercy from them. Yet he avoided the gallows thanks to two pieces of good fortune. First, there was no small black SS blood group tattoo on the underside of his left arm. This was a mark of pride among the members of the elite warrior brotherhood, but its practical purpose was to allow the rapid transfer of blood from one soldier to a wounded comrade in the heat of battle. Although a senior officer, Brunner's duties were almost entirely administrative and carried out far from the Front. As a result, he had never acquired the telltale tattoo that was damning proof of SS membership. That helped him to keep his head down when he was detained in an Allied prison camp in the first months after the war, when the hunt for Nazi war criminals was at its most intense. The Soviets were certainly looking for an Austrian Nazi by the name of A. Brunner, who they knew had been involved in the mass deportation of doomed Jews and other 'undesirables'. They found him, tried him in the People's Court in Prague, and executed him on 24 May 1946. Having dealt with the war criminal *Anton* Brunner, the investigators moved on to the next name on their list.

Many months passed before the Allies realized that two Brunners had worked in the Nazis' Central Office for Jewish Emigration. Colleagues there had known Alois and Anton as Brunner I and Brunner II. Both men were Austrian officers, fervently anti-Semitic and highly regarded by their chief Adolf Eichmann. Both travelled around occupied Europe organizing the forced collection of unwanted communities and their despatch to their designated place of extermination. Both were dedicated officers and highly effective at urging their colleagues to speed things up whenever there seemed to be a lull in the delivery of victims to the camps. Both demonstrated a talent for terrorizing Jewish prisoners by random acts of public sadism in order to ensure their cowed cooperation. Alois's particular dedication to the cause was rewarded in 1943, when he was appointed commander of the collection camp for French Jews at Drancy in northern Paris. He also excelled at hunting down Belgian and Dutch Jews, as well as liberal and left-wing German intellectuals who had taken refuge in Vichy France. After the war, investigators calculated that the two Brunners were jointly responsible for sending more than 220,000 souls into the Nazi death machine.

LYING LOW IN THE LEVANT

Anton Brunner's arrest and execution bought time for lucky Alois, who soon found work as a driver for the US Army in Munich, which in turn helped him to start building a fresh identity and acquiring new papers. By 1947, however, it was clear that the Nazi hunters had realized their mistake and were

Adolf Eichmann's former assistant Alois Brunner sent more than 100,000 Jews to the concentration camps. After the war, he escaped to Egypt, then Damascus in Syria, where he lived until his death.

now actively looking for the missing Brunner, who seemed to have vanished. By then, Alois had become Herr Schmaldienst and was working as a clerk at a colliery near Essen in the Ruhr. In 1954, his name changed again to Dr Georg Fischer, thanks to an SS comrade who passed on his own old and now unwanted identity papers. That summer, Fischer joined the slow caravan of former Nazis making their way along the ratline that led south to Rome in the hope of a fresh passport from the International Red Cross.

His chosen final destination was not in South America, however, but in the Middle East. After a brief spell in Cairo selling munitions, Dr Fischer eventually reappeared in Damascus working in the unpromising post of sales representative for a German brewery in a Muslim country. Fortunately, he was able to earn a second income advising the Syrian secret services.

Syria was a good choice of bolthole for Fischer. During the inter-war years, Syria had been controlled by the French, who had used their military power to crush popular local opposition. In the 1930s, Arab nationalists throughout the Middle East looked to Nazi Germany as a potential ally against their two main colonialist enemies, France and Britain, who controlled Palestine and Egypt. Hitler privately viewed the Arabs as a racially inferior people, but he was happy to offer temporary support to anyone who could be useful in weakening the two Western imperial powers. In the years before the war, Arab leaders were frequently photographed in Berlin and at Berchtesgaden alongside Hitler, Himmler and other Nazi potentates.

Some of that diplomatic warmth remained after the war, enough at least to help more than a hundred Nazis obtain entry passes into the newly independent Syrian state after 1946. Even better, the new government in Damascus refused entry to French war-crime investigators: the Romanian-born Nazi hunter Serge Klarsfeld, whose father had been sent to Auschwitz by Alois Brunner, was barred from Syria on the grounds that he had been educated in France and had become a French citizen.

USEFUL MEN

Events in the tangled history of the region further strengthened the position of former Nazis in the Middle East. Between 1947 and 1949, the Arab states surrounding Palestine failed to stop the establishment of an independent Israel and suffered a series of humiliating military defeats in the process. The governments in Damascus and Cairo recognized the need to strengthen and modernize their military and intelligence capacity. There was no shortage of talented Germans willing to act as mercenary advisers, experienced officers who had fought in a modern technological war, and useful men such as logistic administrators and engineers who knew how to organize one. Typical of these was Walter Rauff, inventor of the mobile gas van, who served as an adviser to Syrian intelligence in late 1948. Rauff worked so closely with the Syrian president that he had to leave in a hurry when the regime suddenly collapsed in the turmoil that followed the catastrophic defeat to Israel the following spring. General Wilhelm Fahrmbacher held high command in the Wehrmacht from the annexation of the Sudetenland in 1938 until the surrender of his last post, the garrison city and submarine base of Lorient in Brittany on 10 August 1945. After his release from Allied custody in 1950, he very quickly found a new position as adviser to the central staff of the Egyptian Army, which he held throughout the 1950s. Fahrmbacher was instrumental in the programme to create an Arab missile force capable of hitting every military target in Israel. Working with him on that project was fellow emigrant Wilhelm Voss, a highly skilled industrial manager who had sat on the boards of almost a dozen armaments companies in the Third Reich. He had also successfully managed the famous Škoda Works in occupied Czechoslovakia.

In the following decade, Hitler's top aircraft designer Willy Messerschmitt worked on another Egyptian weapons project designed to tilt the military balance in the Middle East. Messerschmitt had been imprisoned in the late 1940s for using slave labour in his factories during the war. On his release in 1950, he found that it was forbidden for German businesses to manufacture aeroplanes, so he set about rebuilding his company, making small cars and domestic appliances. In the 1960s, he returned to the aircraft industry, designing a supersonic fighter plane that very much interested the Egyptian President Nasser. The Helwan 300 interceptor made its successful maiden flight for the Egyptian Air Force in 1964. Work on refining it continued for another five years until the Egyptians admitted they could no longer afford the development costs and decided to buy cheaper planes from the Soviet Union instead. German technical expertise was excellent, but it didn't come cheap.

SETTLING DOWN IN SYRIA

Alois Brunner-Fischer wisely stayed on in the Middle East, making himself useful to the Syrian authorities and putting his faith in their reluctance to hand him over to the hated French. His good luck in Damascus continued when he survived two attempts at assassination by letter-bomb in 1961 and 1980, probably gifts from Israeli agents. These explosive packages cost him an eye and several fingers, a small price to pay for living in relative safety in what was then still a very pleasant city. Foreign journalists spotted him relaxing at various hotels and at private receptions, and they noted that he appeared to enjoy personal protection from the Syrian police. Brunner was tried *in absentia* in France on two occasions and found guilty of war crimes, yet attempts at extradition continued to founder. Several Syrian governments claimed that he was not living in their country at all. By the late 1980s, however, the geopolitical atmosphere in the Middle East had changed yet again. It now seemed that Syria was about to give in to years of East German pressure and was finally preparing to hand Brunner over to face trial in Berlin. This time he was saved by history: the Iron Curtain began to crack and East Germany ceased to exist. After 1990, government departments in the suddenly reunified Germany were swamped with new problems and priorities. The dust on Brunner's files began to settle again. As with many Nazis on the run, there were the inevitable rumours that he had moved to South America, but this was unlikely. By then he was an ill, elderly man of increasingly limited means. The only reliable later sightings suggest that, as he grew old, he became much poorer and that he led a shabby, lonely life in Damascus in ever-cheaper accommodation, still spouting his anti-Semitic remarks and justifying his role in the Holocaust to the very end. Nazi hunters and German officials agree that he probably died in the early years of the new century, having successfully evaded justice to the very end.

UNCLE TAREK'S BRIEFCASE

It was an old brown briefcase of the kind that retired college professors carry out of habit. The buckles were rusted, the leather cracked, stained and worn at the edges; it was the last useful possession of an old man whose body had already been disposed of in a cemetery where only the poorest citizens of Cairo ended up. Dangling from the handle of the case, a small rectangular leather tab contained a faded card bearing the owner's name. Inside the case was a tidily organized archive, mostly in brittle yellowed paper, comprising letters, some cancelled bills, faded accounts, medical notes and records, unopened and resealed envelopes bearing European and South American stamps and an unconvincing dark green document confirming the owner's right to reside in Egypt. All were now laid out on a lawyer's dark wooden table. It was all that remained of the owner's life, the life of Tarek Farid Hussein.

Tarek, a tall, tired elderly man, was well known and liked in his world, which consisted of the nearest four or five cramped Cairo streets encircling the small cheap hotel where he lived. In this tiny universe, he did his shopping, sipped his black Ahwa coffee at a table on the street and carefully looked up and down for unfamiliar, inquisitive faces. He seemed a kind man who, as the local street urchins knew, sometimes left a small bonbon behind on the saucer by his drained glass for the first small hand to reach his empty table. He often brought back small pieces of sweet basbousa cake for the Doma family, who were his friendly landlords and whose children came to call him Uncle Tarek. And he was certainly a moral man: he prayed every Friday at the Most Resplendent, the gloriously minareted 10th-century Al-Azhar Mosque linked forever to the Prophet's daughter Fatimah. Above all, he was a man who lived a quiet, private life, taking care to befriend and never offend his neighbours. Clearly, he was not born an Egyptian; his summer tan was too quick to fade in the winter months, his Arabic was broken and limited. But he was a decent man nonetheless, liked and respected by all who knew him. After his death, however, the contents of his briefcase revealed that Tarek had another name from an earlier life, one that he had tried hard to bury in the past: Aribert Ferdinand Heim. A man known as Dr Death in three extermination camps: Mauthausen, Sachsenhausen and Buchenwald.

PAPERWEIGHTS AND POISON

In 1940, Dr Heim, a graduate of the universities of Graz and Vienna, was serving as Captain Heim of the Waffen-SS, attached first to Mauthausen and later to its overflow outpost at Ebensee close to the Führerstadt of Linz. Witnesses who had been in Heim's office at Mauthausen remembered the large paperweight on his desk. A young male inmate had the misfortune to possess a set of perfect teeth cased within an unusual skull, which excited Heim's interest in racial anatomical peculiarities. After being slaughtered and subjected to an unnecessary autopsy that was akin to butchery, the corpse of the young man was decapitated. His boiled and polished head served as a curious conversation piece for Heim's colleagues and visitors. Like a number of Nazi 'doctors', Heim was interested in the extremes of human endurance, and at the Mauthausen complex he had the opportunity and unchallenged authority to perform a series of inhuman surgical procedures. Prison inmates underwent internal 'experiments' without anaesthesia. Organs were removed in order to observe how the victim's body coped, and to measure the speed at which death ensued. Random chemical substances such as poison, bleaches and petroleum were injected into the bloodstream or directly into critical organs. After a brief period of detention and superficial questioning by the US Army in 1945, Heim built a reputation as a well-regarded gynaecologist in the Black Forest spa town of Baden-Baden. He avoided justice in 1962 by disappearing just in time after a telephone tip-off alerted him that the net was closing.

GONE TO GROUND

Heim became one of the most sought-after war criminals in the following decades, thanks in part to his press nickname, the 'Butcher of Mauthausen'. For the next 30 years, Nazi hunters and the Western press looked for him in all the usual places in Spain and South America. Periodically, there were less credible claims that he was now living in Scandinavia or California. There were hints that he had escaped from Spain to Morocco with help from Hitler's top commando, Otto Skorzeny. Then it was said that he had made his way onwards to Egypt via Tunis, but this was dismissed as a deliberate red herring. In fact, like other Nazi fugitives, Heim had seen the advantages that hiding in Egypt offered. Like Syria in the late 1940s and 1950s, it was a relatively welcoming destination for Germans of a certain experience and background. The monarch, King Farouk, resented British influence in his country and the surrounding region. Although Egypt had been nominally independent since 1922, the British continued to maintain a significant military force there to ensure their control of the Suez Canal and the vital link to British India. After 1945, Farouk was keen to promote German-Egyptian relations as a way of signalling his independence from London. German experts were engaged to help train the Egyptian air force. Others were recruited for their experience as anti-Jewish propagandists, which might make them useful in the struggle against Israel. Under Farouk and then the nationalist leader General Nasser, several former Nazis headed up joint information organizations such as the Friends of Cairo and the Arab-German Friendship League.

While Western eyes scoured South America for missing war criminals, the Russian and East German intelligence services were much more aware of the presence of wanted men like Heim in places such as Egypt, but they also knew that any extradition requests would always be politely refused. In the 1960s, the West German government briefly investigated a rumour that Heim was working as a doctor for the Egyptian police, but closed the file for lack of evidence. Heim went on to live out the rest of his life in Cairo without detection and with little fear of being brought to justice. By taking an Arab name, converting to Islam and most importantly keeping clear of all other Germans in the city, he vanished under the radar. His strategy only came to light in 2009, when his son admitted that he had frequently carried money from Heim's sister in Germany over to Cairo. He had also been with his father when he died of cancer in 1992. Tarek's briefcase, looked after by the loyal Doma family for 18 years, was finally reopened. Documents in the case confirmed the son's claims. And it contained an unsent letter to the German news magazine *Der Spiegel*, written in Heim's hand, protesting his innocence and accusing the Jew Simon Wiesenthal of making up all the tales about his supposed medical atrocities. The contents of the briefcase revealed that Tarek, the good Muslim, remained a virulent anti-Semite and a proud admirer and defender of Adolf Hitler until the very end.

SHELTERING BEHIND THE SHAMROCK

Far to the west of the dry lands of the Middle East, many Nazis found lusher, greener pastures in which to spend the post-war years. In the heart of County Kildare and close by the Curragh,

Benito Mussolini is rescued from captivity by German paratroopers in Campo Imperatore, Italy, September 1943. Otto Skorzeny (with moustache) is immediately to his left.

the spiritual home of Irish horse racing, there stands an attractive 19th-century country home fit for any gentleman. Decorated in a light Gothic style, it was commissioned in the 1830s by the third Duke of Leinster as a shooting lodge, although it was, of course, said that he really used it as a quiet location to meet with his mistress(es). By 1959, however, the Leinster family had lost much of its wealth. That year, Martinstown House and its remaining estate of 165 acres acquired a new owner. Although in his early 50s, he was an imposing and dynamic man, well over six foot tall and powerfully built. The long fencing scar that ran across his left cheek and his white Mercedes marked him out from the other landowners in the county. He made no attempt to disguise his identity and felt no need to do so. For Otto Skorzeny, formerly a member of Hitler's elite bodyguard and once described in the British press as 'the most dangerous man in Europe', felt quite at home with his new life as a gentleman farmer in the Republic of Ireland.

Skorzeny was an Austrian who joined the Nazi movement in 1931, long before his country was annexed by Hitler. A member of the SA and then the SS, he built a reputation as a highly competent and inspiring officer on the Eastern Front. In April 1943, Skorzeny was appointed commander of an SS special operations unit charged with anti-partisan activities and conducting sabotage behind enemy lines. Five months later, he came to global attention thanks to his part in Operation Oak, the German mission to locate and liberate the fallen dictator Mussolini, who had been arrested by Italy's new pro-Allied government. Skorzeny and 16 SS comrades were part of a German glider force that set off from Rome on 12 September and landed on the high meadows of Campo Imperatore in the mountains of Abruzzo. Although he was not the officer commanding the mission, Skorzeny ensured that his men were the first to arrive at the remote ski hotel where *Il Duce* (The Leader) was being held under guard. Skorzeny also made sure that he featured prominently in the SS photographs recording the daring escapade, and that he accompanied Mussolini on the light Fieseler Storch used to convey him down from the mountains and to safety. Propaganda Minister Goebbels made the most of this dramatic success, presenting Skorzeny to the war-weary German public as a model hero of the Reich. Other missions that Skorzeny led – to kidnap Marshall Tito at his headquarters in Drvar in the Bosnian part of Yugoslavia, to sabotage Allied supply lines in Iran and to assassinate Stalin, Roosevelt and Churchill when they met in Teheran – were much less fruitful, yet Hitler retained confidence in his 'top commando' throughout the rest of the war.

EXONERATED AND DENAZIFIED

As a resourceful and ruthless commando, Skorzeny's actions and orders almost inevitably transgressed the strict letter of international law on the waging of war. As a result, he faced a war crimes tribunal at Dachau in 1947, called to account for his conduct during the Battle of the Bulge in the Ardennes in late 1944. Ordered to confuse and destabilize the enemy, several small groups of Skorzeny's English-speaking men had infiltrated Allied lines wearing US and British uniforms and driving US Army vehicles. Senior Wehrmacht officers had always condemned this guerrilla tactic: troops who fell into enemy hands 'disguised' in this way forfeited any hope of protection from the Geneva Convention. In the event, 18 of Skorzeny's men captured in Allied uniforms were shot as spies. However, after a war crimes trial lasting three weeks, their commander escaped the executioner on a fine legal point; it was conceded that his men had worn Allied uniforms only in order to deceive their enemy. There was no concrete evidence that they had been ordered to engage in combat while dressed as GIs or Tommies.

Although acquitted, Skorzeny remained in Allied custody, as it was expected that he would soon be prosecuted for crimes committed during his tours of duty in Eastern Europe. Ironically, in 1948 he was spirited away from an American internment camp near Darmstadt by three former SS comrades masquerading as US military policemen. Over the next few years, Skorzeny was spotted in Paris, Madrid and Cairo. He was also thought to have been working for Juan and Eva Perón in Buenos Aires, supervising their security arrangements. In the changed climate of the Cold War, he was eventually reclassified as 'denazified' in 1952, and therefore able to apply for an Austrian passport. This helped him not only to travel at will around Europe, but also to buy rather expensive properties in Majorca and in Ireland.

AT HOME IN IRELAND

Skorzeny claimed that he purchased Martinstown House because he planned to buy and train racehorses there. The Irish National Stud was, after all, merely five miles away from his new property. Probably the real reason for his settling in the Republic was the warm welcome he had received in Dublin two years before. Well into the 1950s, memories of the Irish War of Independence were still raw and anti-British sentiment was still strong. Officially, Ireland remained strictly neutral between 1939 and 1945, refusing to allow British naval access to its ports and referring to the war that engulfed Europe in those years by its own parochial term, the Emergency. Éamon de Valera, Taoiseach or premier, used the war as an opportunity to reinforce the new Ireland's separateness from Britain and emphasize its independence from British foreign policy. Many of the 60,000 Irish men and women who fought against Hitler in the British Armed Forces later commented on the cold reception they received when they returned home after the war. By contrast, Skorzeny was feted at a dinner held in his honour at the golf resort of Portmarnock in 1957, where he met many of the movers and shakers in Irish society. Most, though not all, Irish journalists and commentators who recorded his presence in the Republic were happy to portray him as a glamorous, daring warrior, but they made little reference to the regime that he had served. Until he sold up and moved to Madrid in 1969, Skorzeny was a familiar if quite distant figure in Kildare, who went about his business without fear or hindrance. He probably left Ireland just in time, for Irish attitudes to the war began to change in the 1970s as public understanding of the Holocaust deepened. Skorzeny's own involvement in the arrest and elimination of the Stauffenberg plotters in 1944 also became better known.

A HUNDRED WELCOMES

More than a hundred Nazis took advantage of the possibility to build a new life in Ireland in the first decades after the war. The most prominent of these was Albert Folens, who founded the highly successful educational publishing company that still bears his name, and who continued to live in the Republic until his death in 2003. When Belgium was occupied in 1940, Folens was 23 years old and a passionate Flemish nationalist. He believed that Hitler was sympathetic to the idea of Flemish independence from French-speaking Brussels. A highly educated young man who was a voracious reader, his study of Russian history since 1917 had also made him profoundly anti-communist. As a result, he joined the Waffen-SS Flemish Legion, believing that it was his duty to fight Stalinism and hoping that this small volunteer force could be the core of a future Flemish national army. Under different names and formats, the Legion fought throughout the war on the Eastern Front until its battered remnants surrendered to the Red Army in Mecklenburg on 8 May 1945. Folens missed all the action, however, due to serious ill health. Instead, he spent most of the occupation years doing secretarial and translation work at the Gestapo HQ in Brussels. As a consequence, he was listed in the Nazi hunters' bible, the Central Registry of War Criminals and Security Suspects (CROWCASS), and arrested by the British. There was no evidence that he had been directly involved in any acts of torture or murder, but, like many Flemish nationalists, he was found guilty of the crime of collaboration. After serving 31 months of a 10-year sentence, he miraculously escaped detention. With the aid of a group of Belgian Trappist monks and a false passport, he was one of a group of 25 Flemish Nazi refugees smuggled out of Belgium and into Ireland. Already fluent in several languages, he quickly mastered Irish and integrated into the cultural life of the Republic. In 1957, he founded the very successful publishing house that at one stage operated not just in Ireland but also in Great Britain and several Central European states. Critics of some of its history schoolbooks, however, noted a tendency to skim over many aspects of the Nazi period.

FIGHTING FRANCE

As a chemist, making a bomb was a relatively simple task for Célestin Lainé. This particular bomb was not the first explosive device he had made. Satisfied that his handiwork was complete, he put the device in a small box, put it all in a bag and handed it to his co-conspirator. Later that morning, 7 August 1932, the bomb did its job. The detested statue in the main square of Rennes, which commemorated the absorption of independent Brittany into France exactly 400 years before, had been obliterated.

The path taken by Lainé into long exile in Ireland was similar in some respects to that of Albert Folens. Lainé was also an intellectual and a cultural nationalist. In his case, the hated cultural oppressor was France, but he also hoped that supporting Hitler might spark opportunities for freeing his beloved Breton people. His path, however, was significantly more violent. Impressed by the success of the IRA, throughout the 1930s Lainé attempted to construct a similar paramilitary organization, but to little effect. Thanks to the confusion of occupation, however, by 1943 he had finally managed to create and equip a group of a hundred or so activists known as the Perrot Militia in honour of Jean-Marie Perrot, a Breton nationalist priest who had been murdered by the French Resistance. This seed of a future Breton liberation army wore grey-green German uniforms, acted as auxiliaries for the Gestapo and took part in actions against the Breton Maquis. As so often in brutal wars that involve civilians, old scores were settled and sadistic appetites indulged. Loyalist families and those with Resistance connections were at the top of Lainé's hit list. He specialized in rounding up the young men and women of 'suspected' families and throwing their tortured bodies into mass graves in the Breton woods once his men were finished with them.

The following summer, as the Allies swept on towards Paris, the men of the Perrot Militia burned their German uniforms and went to ground. Some headed for the Reich, hoping to disappear in the Black Forest, but this soon proved to be a mistake that inevitably led to capture by the French authorities and the severest punishment. Lainé himself abandoned his remaining men in early June 1944, just as they were about to be rounded up and shot. He secretly made his way to Ireland and eventually settled in County Galway, where he lived quietly and made a living as a chemist. He was sentenced to death *in absentia* by the French authorities, but was essentially ignored by the Irish. For the next 40 years, he immersed himself in pan-Celtic mysticism, dreaming of a united commonwealth of the ancient Celtic peoples along the Atlantic seaboard. Until his death in 1983, however, he could never relax. He feared the day when one of his enemies would come down along the road – an

Allied investigator, a gunman from the Resistance, or one of his own former Breton militia colleagues who had sworn to avenge the comrades he had betrayed.

STOPPING OFF IN DUBLIN

The village of Rathgar was once a picturesque halt on the road in and out of the Irish capital. Swallowed up by the city long ago, it became a leafy suburb of red-brick Georgian and Victorian terraces much appreciated by the city's upper middle classes. In the great age of ecclesiastical building, one of Rathgar's places of worship was nicknamed 'the servant's church', on account of its large congregation of domestic staff who lived and worked within the area's imposing housing stock. Famous names such as James Joyce and Bram Stoker were Rathgar residents. And for a brief moment in 1947, sedate Rathgar was also home to one of the most wanted men in Europe: Andrija Artuković, also known as the 'Butcher of the Balkans'.

Artuković was a qualified lawyer and an early member of the militant Croatian nationalist organization, the fascistic Ustaše. From the foundation of the movement in 1929, he was involved in a range of subversive and violent activities in inter-war Yugoslavia until he was obliged to go into exile in 1932. As he wandered throughout Europe in the 1930s, he inspired and organized several terrorist outrages by Croatian émigrés. As a notorious agitator, he came to the attention of national security services and consequently spent time in prisons in Belgrade, Budapest, Vienna, London and Paris. He even disturbed the Gestapo, who considered locking him up when he passed through Berlin in 1937. The Nazis were impressed by his energy and fanaticism, however, and remembered him when Hitler invaded and dismembered Yugoslavia in 1941.

They immediately handed control of their new puppet state of Croatia to Ante Pavelić, the leader of the Ustaše. And they approved of his appointment of Artuković as interior minister in charge of security, public order and later justice and religious affairs. Artuković controlled all the levers needed to realize the Ustaše dream of a racially and ideologically 'pure' Croatia. All the usual mechanisms of a modern totalitarian state were at his disposal: control of the official and the secret police organizations, a punitive judicial system, killing squads and detention camps. As ever, the target victims included the Jews and the Romani, but like most of the Ustaše, Artuković particularly detested Orthodox Christian Serbs. His first action was to remove all unreliable and unwanted peoples from any position of authority or influence within the new Croatia. Jews, Serbs and those democratically minded Croats who did not share the dream of a racialist state were sacked and replaced by Ustaše members and fellow travellers. Then the physical persecution of the undesirable minorities began in earnest.

Even by the horrific standards of World War II, the atrocities committed in the Balkans were hellish. The Ustaše were not especially anti-Semitic, but were happy to murder Jews to keep their Nazi allies content. Their own particular form of hatred was fuelled more by the racial and religious antagonisms that had long festered throughout the bloody history of the Balkans. The Scottish soldier and spy Fitzroy Maclean was active in wartime Yugoslavia and later remembered witnessing the awful results of Ustaše bloodlust, the medieval carnage in the smaller villages and the trophy displays of Serb body parts even in the streets of the capital Zagreb. Inevitably, the majority of victims were those too young or too old to flee or fight. German officers serving in the Balkans complained to Berlin that even their battle-hardened troops had been sickened and demoralized by what they discovered in towns that had been visited by Ustaše terror squads. In the Croatian concentration camps, thousands succumbed to the usual hazards of starvation, exhaustion and typhus. However, those who were actually murdered there found that Ustaše operatives were every bit as bestial as guards in German-run camps, and often more so, if that were possible. Rather than the organized, industrial mass murder that befell so many victims of the Third Reich, death at the hands of the Ustaše in places such as Jasenovac was usually a more personal, hands-on affair. Prisoners were quite casually despatched individually by axe, mallet, heavy iron mace or by the *srbosjek* or Serb-cutter, a leather glove with a curved knife attached that was originally used by butchers and huntsmen. It was ideal for slitting throats quickly and deeply. Survivors told of mass hangings where the victims were quartered as they dangled half-alive on the gallows before tumbling into the pits below. Others reported that the guards held throat-slitting competitions to see how many prisoners could be killed in the allotted time.

Gradually, the charge sheet against Artuković built up; he was the government minister principally responsible for organizing and facilitating these atrocities. But it also listed specific inhuman incidents that were not just committed under his administrative watch, but were events in which he was directly implicated and at which he was sometimes present. The entire populations of numerous villages suspected of sheltering partisans were liquidated by his personal order, as were the prisoners at Tepec Hill in 1943, where the victims were gunned down and their bodies crushed and pressed into the earth under tank tracks.

When the Croatian puppet state collapsed in May 1945, Artuković fell into Allied hands, but by late 1946 he and his family had made it into neutral Switzerland under a false name. When his true identity was revealed in July 1947, the angry and embarrassed Swiss authorities bundled him out of the country on a plane. It was bound for Ireland, the only country willing to help the Swiss take care of their 'predicament'. Artuković spent a very pleasant and unmolested year in Rathgar, where he posed as a displaced history professor and made a very positive impression in the local community. During that year in Dublin, the political climate in Europe changed, rage at wartime events cooled a little more, and the dust of time slowly began to cover the tracks of many guilty men.

When it was appropriate, Artuković and his family decamped to California, where he remained for 38 years despite being a known war criminal and having only an expired tourist visa to support his long presence in the US. Yugoslav extradition requests were repeatedly frustrated, thanks to political pressure from the Croatian émigré community in the US and the influence of James McIntyre, a conservative and controversial Roman Catholic Archbishop of Los Angeles. The fact that post-war Yugoslavia was now communist served in his favour. Belgrade made its first extradition request in 1951, at the height of the Cold War. In that climate, it was easy for his defending lawyers to argue that Artuković would never get a fair trial from Marshal Tito, and 'should not be sent back to certain death at the hands of the Reds'. It was only in the much-changed political climate of the 1980s that he was finally returned to Europe to face justice. In 1986, he was tried in Zagreb, found guilty of mass murder and condemned to death. By then 88 years old, physically ill, afflicted by dementia and weighing little more than six stone, his lawyers won him a stay of execution. He was found dead in his prison hospital bed in January 1988. He never admitted his guilt and never expressed regret for his actions. His son said that his father was 'only guilty of having been on the losing side in World War II'.

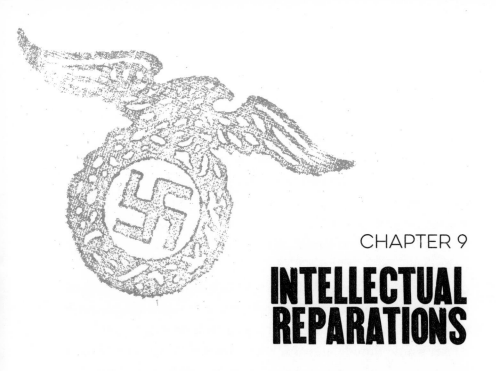

CHAPTER 9

INTELLECTUAL REPARATIONS

'I was in a boarding house, I think it was about January 1945 or so and one of these V-2 rockets came in and hit a building about two blocks away and smashed our house and threw me out of the john into the hallway. I remember as I came out of my jolting stupor, the landlady screaming, you know. And I'm never sure whether she was screaming at the sight of me with very little clothing on or the fact that half her house was gone... Whole areas of that city were gone and you'd come off the tube and there were people sleeping in the platform because they had nowhere else to go... I think if the V-2 attacks had kept on, if our army hadn't captured the sites, there may have been a breaking point there. The V-1, you could hear it coming over and you could watch it coming, then when the motor cut out, it would fall, then change direction and go down and you knew something was coming in. The V-2, you didn't. It hit, and a section of the city disappeared. It was an unbelievable weapon,' remembered Canadian navy veteran Gerald Bowen, on shore leave in London at the time.

First launched on London on 8 September 1944, the 'Vengeance Weapon Two' (V-2), as it was called by Goebbels' Propaganda Ministry in reference to the unending Allied bombing campaign on German cities, carried a 2,200-lb (997 kg) warhead travelling at 2,500 miles per hour (4,000 km/h) with a range of 200 miles (322 km). Using rocket technology, the world's first ballistic missile would launch vertically, its engine only firing for a minute. Gyroscopes would then tilt it to 45 degrees, at which it travelled up for 50 miles until it reached the very edge of space. An accelerometer would then ensure that the engine cut at the right speed to locate its target. The rocket would tumble in space, but its fins kept the nose pointing forwards as it re-entered the atmosphere. Flying too high and too fast to be intercepted, and making little or no sound because it flew faster than the speed of sound, it would hit the ground at over 1,500 miles per hour (2,414 km/h) before exploding and causing extensive damage and death. Although too little and too late to prevent defeat in World War II, this sophisticated technology did not go unnoticed.

The V-2 was only one of a number of impressive developments in military technology brought about by German scientists; others were in biological weaponry, such as disease and nerve agents like sarin, a bubonic plague weapon, the development of nuclear technology, as well as tank armour, aircraft propulsion systems and even stealth technology. The Allies were also keen to exploit Germany's industrial assets. Although in retrospect some say that the Allies' belief in the extent and effectiveness of Nazi technology was exaggerated, they were desperate to get access to Nazi German scientists, physicists and engineers, along with weapons, machinery and documentation – not only to give themselves an economic and commercial edge, but also to prevent those advantages from falling into Soviet hands.

THE SCRAMBLE FOR SECRETS

Armed with the experiences of the end of World War I and the adverse effect of expecting billions of dollars to be paid in compensation by a nation defeated in a devastating conflict, the US Congress gave the president authorization to enable any country whose defence he defined as 'vital to the United States' to receive arms, other equipment and material 'by sale, transfer, exchange or lease' as early as March 1941, in preparation for the issue of war debts and reparations resulting from World War II. Detailed discussions on the matter began at the Yalta Conference in February 1945, with the formation of a reparations commission. In conclusion, the commission suggested reparations worth $20 billion (in equipment, machine-tools, ships, rolling stocks, etc., annual deliveries of goods from current production for a period to be fixed, as well as the use of German labour) of which the USSR would receive 50 per cent. Matters were finalized at Potsdam in July, two months after the German surrender.

By then, though, black operations on reparations were already well under way. As early as November 1944, Allied experts in biological weapons were recorded in Strasbourg, studying documents left behind by Dr Eugen Haagen, an expert in weaponizing deadly viruses. They also uncovered evidence that Haagen had been conducting his experiments on concentration camp prisoners. Other names mentioned in these documents were the Third Reich's surgeon general Walter Schreiber and his deputy Dr Kurt Blome. All three names went on the wanted list – scientists who desired to live and work in the United States! Although the US authorities were concerned about Germany's post-war economic recovery, they began a campaign of industrial espionage, procuring chemical patents, machine tools and German technological information.

For their part, the Soviets were not inactive. Even before Potsdam, they had begun to dismantle whole German industrial plants and transport them to Soviet territory. Their plan was to prevent any German recovery by extracting maximum reparations as quickly as possible, and by using the four million German POWs in its territories as forced labour to rebuild and stabilize their own economy.

The end of hostilities saw the start of a scramble for Nazi German scientific secrets. In what turned out to be the first days of the Cold War, the US and the Soviet Union found themselves in a race against time and against each other. In March 1945, the Allies hit pay dirt when a Polish lab technician found a list of names stuffed into a toilet at Bonn University. This turned out to be a list of scientists, engineers and technicians recalled from combat duty by Hitler in 1943 to assist in the war effort. The list was compiled by Werner Osenberg, and included what were regarded as the Third Reich's top scientific minds. The list reached British and finally US intelligence, becoming the basis for their recruitment effort.

The race continued. In April 1945, the US launched Operation Lusty to evaluate the Luftwaffe's secret aeronautical technology. In May, Red Army troops took over the atomic research labs at the Kaiser Wilhelm Institute in the suburbs of Berlin, which provided them with what would become the key to unlocking the vast Soviet nuclear arsenal. At almost the same time, the USS *Sutton*, a US Navy destroyer, captured a German U-boat off Newfoundland. On board the *U-234*, they found Dr

Heinz Schlicke, Director of Naval Test Fields at Kiel and an expert in electronic warfare. The cargo included plans for the Hs 293 glider bomb, the V-1 glide bomb (forerunner of Cruise missiles), V-2 rocket (forerunner of SCUD missiles), the Me 262 fighter aircraft (the first combat jet fighter), low observable submarine designs and lead-lined boxes filled with 1,200 lbs (544 kg) of uranium oxide, a key ingredient of atomic bombs.

As Allied and Soviet troops and intelligence services combed the European countryside in search of any hidden caches of weaponry they could find, it soon became clear that simply studying the weapons was not enough; they needed the scientists too.

NEW RECRUITS

The first hits for the Allies continued to come easily. Number 1 on America's so-called *Black List* of desired Nazi rocket scientists, Wernher von Braun – inventor of the V-2 – surrendered to US forces on 2 May, bringing a number of his colleagues and 14 tons of documents with him. They had left their base at Peenemünde, on the Baltic coast of eastern Germany, a few days before the Soviets arrived to capture it. As von Braun had expected, they were welcomed with open arms, safe in the knowledge that what they knew was more important to the Allies than what they had done for Nazi Germany. Von Braun and a number of his technicians arrived at Fort Strong on the northern tip of Boston Harbour's Long Island, the processing point for their entry into the US, on 20 September.

The British, too, were busy in this field. They designed a programme aimed at exploiting German scientific and technical know-how, using scientists and technicians as 'human booty' to give Britain advantages not only in military matters but also

Inventors of the German V-2 rocket, Professor Wernher von Braun (l, arm in a cast) and his brother Magnus, after they surrendered to US 7th Army troops in the Alps, May 1945. Von Braun's arm and shoulder were fractured in a car crash a few weeks before, when his driver fell asleep at the wheel.

in industry and commerce. In the last months of the war, the Alsos Mission, an Allied effort to find out if the Germans had an atomic bomb programme, captured Werner Heisenberg at a nuclear facility near Württemberg. He was the principal scientist in the Nazi nuclear weapons programme. In June 1945, on the instruction of MI6, they undertook an 'enforced evacuation' of 50 scientists and technicians from their homes in Magdeburg. Organized by the British Intelligence Objectives Sub-Committee (BIOS), the operation was carried out by a British Army field unit known as T-Force. The kidnap victims, snatched against their will, included aircraft designers, experts in underwater acoustics, electron microscopes, munitions and sarin gas. Another notable early success was engineer Hellmuth Walter, who pioneered hydrogen peroxide propulsion systems for aeroplanes, submarines and rockets. Other such missions were also carried out by an Anglo-American military intelligence unit called the Field Information Agency (Technical) or FIAT. In an effort to make these operations as efficient as possible, the Allies had organized luxurious accommodation for their captives in advance of their deportation. One, the Palace Hotel in Luxembourg, was codenamed 'Ashcan'; the other, Crane Mountain Castle in Hesse, Germany, was dubbed 'Dustbin'.

OPERATION PAPERCLIP

In August 1945, President Truman authorized the dropping of atomic bombs on the Japanese cities of Hiroshima and Nagasaki, marking the end of all hostilities and sending the scramble for nuclear capability into overdrive. In response to rising tensions, the US Department of Defense issued a warning of the need to prepare for atomic, chemical and biological war with Russia, which might start at early as 1952. Its top-secret recruitment of

Nazi scientists was officially sanctioned as Operation Overcast. Although the president was not informed at first, the operation was high up the chain, briefed by the Joint Intelligence Committee and run by the Joint Intelligence Objectives Agency (JOIA) and the Office of Strategic Services (OSS), forerunner of the CIA.

The early successes of the US operation continued. As well as von Braun, they 'recruited' other eminent members of the V-2 team, including engineers Arthur Rudolph, Kurt Debus and Bernhard Tessmann. These names were added to a list that already featured the nuclear physicist Peter Debye, biologist Dr Kurt Blome, aircraft designer Robert Lusser, chemist Walter Reppe and engineer Georg Rickhey. But there were problems. As early as May 1945, *Life* magazine published a photo story with details of the horrors uncovered by Allied troops who liberated the concentration camps, and stories of Nazi escapes to South America. This horrific information was compounded by press coverage of the Nuremberg Trials that began in November 1945. Details of Nazi atrocities and, in particular, the systematic murder of the Jews, outraged the American public and even some members of the War Department. The American operation would be in danger if word got out.

Towards the end of 1945, President Truman was made aware of the initiative. He was concerned about how the inclusion of Nazis in the programme would play with public opinion. He insisted that the scientists should only be allowed to stay temporarily, and that the government should emphasize how useful their contributions were to life in America. The name of the initiative was changed to Operation Paperclip, in reference to paperclips that were attached to the files of those whose pasts were to be kept under wraps.

Despite the president's misgivings, the operation continued to recruit Nazis known to have taken part in war crimes. Members of JIOA, the OSS and the military did what they could to whitewash the real stories of their new recruits by destroying documents in their files, rewriting dossiers and generally 'polishing' their histories, but they had a lot of work to do. Von Braun had been a member of the SS and had visited the concentration camp at Buchenwald to hand-pick slave labourers for the V-2 project; Arthur Rudolph had used workers from the Mittelbau-Dora camp for his work, of which between 12,000 and 20,000 had died of disease, starvation or malnutrition. Others were worked to death or hanged publicly for minor transgressions. Hubertus Strughold had been a part of horrific war crimes during his time as a doctor at Dachau, when he had overseen painful and often fatal experiments on prisoners that involved locking them in pressure chambers and ice-water tanks.

By January 1946, there were some 160 German scientists in the US, some at Hilltop in Dayton, Ohio, where they worked in motor research, aerodynamics, rocket fuels, supersonics and business, and the others, including the rocket scientists, at Fort Bliss in Texas and White Sands Proving Grounds in New Mexico, where they worked alongside US military scientists.

In October 1946, the Soviets struck back with Operation Osoaviakhim, during which police and army units arrested some 2,200 German specialists in aviation, rocketry, communications, agricultural machinery and shipbuilding, and their families who lived in the Soviet occupation zone. They were immediately transported by train, some 6,000 people in all, to various secret locations in Russia. Tons of machinery and other equipment was also transported, particularly from the V-2 rocket centre at Mittelwerk armaments factory in Nordhausen, which was captured after von Braun and his staff had left, and the Luftwaffe's central military aviation test centre at Mecklenburg.

In November 1946, news broke in the US that another thousand or so scientists were on their way from Germany. Newspapers such as the *New York Times* and magazines such as *Newsweek* picked up the story of Operation Paperclip. Public figures, such as former First Lady Eleanor Roosevelt, Albert Einstein and prominent New York rabbi Steven Wise publicly criticized the programme. To counter this, the government issued press reports explaining that the mild-mannered, silver-haired scientists pictured in the newspapers in their American sports jackets had not been real Nazis, merely their victims. Photos were published of the men with their families, hiking, fishing and playing golf in the midst of American landscapes. The ethical debate continued.

ROCKET MAN

Although the British were mainly concerned with learning the secrets of German commerce and industry, they were also interested in the Germans' knowledge of armaments and chemical warfare. It was reported that in 1946 they listed seven scientists from the IG Farben chemical plant whom they were keen to interrogate. It is also known that the BIOS teams sent to track down the scientists or technicians concerned often included representatives from British firms, such as ICI, Pears Soap, Max Factor and Yardley, among others.

However, the policies of the War Department began to be questioned. There were complaints that many of the scientists were being interned in camps, in Germany and in Britain, and were being transported to Britain against their will, often without their families and without money. Of course, there was also the question of their Nazi links to consider, too.

By the summer of 1947, the government began to issue formal employment contracts to these 'guest' workers. Although officially claiming that they would not employ those with 'politically undesirable' backgrounds, there is little evidence that this policy was adhered to. In the event, the British Operation Surgeon identified some 1,500 German scientists and technicians whom they wanted from Germany. In 1947, it is reported that over a hundred of them were employed in Britain, with most of the others finding work in British Commonwealth countries, as well as Sweden, Switzerland, Brazil and South America.

Although the French were as keen as the other Allies to make use of German science and technology, they went about the job in a different way. The Soviets were the least subtle, taking the scientists, the technicians and their laboratories with them to Russia. The US and Britain did a similar thing, taking the personnel away from their homes, but putting them to work in existing state-of-the-art facilities. But the French, perhaps bearing in mind the importance for future cooperation with their neighbours, came up with a different policy. Following initial animosity, which saw similar tactics used by the French military in seizing information and equipment for use in aeronautics and electronics, the French government realized the need for collaboration. German laboratories in the French Occupation Zone became collaborative institutions where French scientists learned German skills and knowledge. This produced mutually beneficial and reliable results, with the added benefit that it was politically acceptable. It might also be judged as valuable in terms of building future relationships between the two nations.

Obsessed with rocketry since the age of 13, Wernher von Braun left school early to pursue his dreams of space travel. In 1932, aged 20, he was offered money by the German army to investigate the possible application of rockets for the military, and began work at the Kummersdorf rocket station south of Berlin. Within three years, his group had developed and launched rockets with liquid-fuelled engines, a new technology that became the basis of modern spaceflight.

In 1942, he finally produced the A-4 missile, which was soon followed by the V-2. Tested at the rocket facility at Peenemünde, the rockets were built at Mittelwerk in central Germany. At some point during these years, von Braun had joined the Nazi Party, the army and the SS – actions that would later cast their shadow on his new life in America.

MOONSHOT

After four years in New Mexico, von Braun and his team were moved to Huntsville, Alabama. In 1953, they delivered the Redstone, America's first ballistic missile, which could deliver a nuclear warhead to a target 250 miles (400 km) away. Five years later came the Jupiter-C, which launched the first US satellite.

With rockets, satellites and atomic bombs now all part of everyday life, the American public soon developed an appetite for science fiction stories and films portraying warriors in outer space, fighting creatures with their ray guns. As the fantasy of the space race began to seem credible, publicity began to shine a light on the suave, sharp-suited, well-spoken von Braun. In 1953, von Braun was given the chance to tell the general public about his plans for manned space travel when he was commissioned to write a series of articles on the subject in *Collier's* magazine. The magazine's circulation soared to four million copies, as readers were fascinated by von Braun's vision of the future. Two years later, Walt Disney asked von Braun to act as technical advisor on a series of space-related films that were to help promote his new Disneyland theme park in California. In fact, the three films were a sensation. Disney himself described the first film, aired in March 1955, as 'science factual'. The series combined real science, presented by the genial and camera-friendly von Braun, and Disney's playful, technically brilliant animation to explain how America was going to go to the Moon and even on to Mars by means of rockets and an orbital space station. An estimated 42 million people watched the opening programme, 'Man in Space', of which one reviewer said, 'Into it went the thinking of the best scientific minds working on space projects today, making the picture more fact than fantasy.'

Von Braun was featured on the cover of *TIME* magazine in 1958, and two years later his rocket group became part of the National Aeronautics and Space Administration (NASA), whose primary objective was to develop giant Saturn rockets. Von Braun was made director of NASA's Marshall Space Flight Center and was the chief architect of the Saturn 5 launch vehicle, the super-booster that would propel man to the Moon.

On 5 May 1961, the first American astronaut, Alan Shepard, made a successful suborbital flight on a Redstone-Mercury rocket built by von Braun's group. Shortly afterwards, the newly elected US president John F. Kennedy, worried that the Soviets were ahead in the space race because of Yuri Gagarin's orbit of the Earth in April 1961, asked Congress to fund a programme to land a man on the Moon by the end of the 1960s.

For the next decade, von Braun was photographed with fellow scientists, astronauts, celebrities and presidents, all in front of the massive rockets he was creating. He took his place in the firing room of the Kennedy Spaceflight Center on Wednesday 16 July 1969 as his Saturn 5 rocket took the Apollo 11 crew to the Moon, thus fulfilling both President Kennedy's mission and his own lifelong dream.

THE 'UNLUCKY ONE'

Working on the Saturn V launch vehicle alongside von Braun during these years were over a hundred of his German colleagues, many of them known by the US authorities to be Nazis. The team included Arthur Rudolph, Hubertus Strughold and Kurt Debus. Rudolph, described in his US intelligence file as '100 per cent Nazi, dangerous type', led the team that built the rocket. Kurt Debus, another ardent member of the Nazi Party – 'He should be interned as a menace to the security of the Allied Forces' – was the head of the Launch Operations Center at Cape Canaveral, while Strughold, later known as the 'father of space medicine' because he designed NASA's on-board life-support systems, had been involved in conducting 'experiments' at Dachau and Auschwitz. Another prominent member of the group, Bernhard Tessmann, who designed the Vertical Assembly Building that housed the rocket before it was launched, was former Facilities Designer at the German missile centre in Peenemünde. The War Department had done their cover-up work well. Although there had been a little opposition to the arrival of the German scientists in 1947, following the intensification of the Cold War it pretty much went away.

Undoubtedly one of the most influential rocket engineers of the 20th century, von Braun had always been lucky. Born to a family of high standing, raised in a privileged environment, supremely gifted academically and able to spend his life paid handsomely for indulging his obsession with rocketry, he died

John F. Kennedy at Cape Canaveral (now Cape Kennedy) with German-born rocket scientist and NASA launch operations director Kurt Debus. Debus was a fanatical Nazi and former SS officer.

in 1977 and was celebrated as a scientific genius and the creator of Saturn V, rather than a Nazi held accountable for what some saw as his war crimes. In an article in *TIME* magazine published in 2019, journalist Alejandro de la Garza summed it up as follows: '[That von Braun] died a largely unquestioned American hero speaks to what was perhaps his greatest skill: salesmanship. To survive in Nazi Germany, he sold Hitler a dream of victory through superior technology. Later, he sold the US Army a vision of intercontinental nuclear dominance. But von Braun's biggest sale of all is apparent in that Disney footage. To Americans, he sold the dream of men in space and flags on the Moon. And by and large, the nation bought it, no questions asked.'

Others were lucky, too. Robert Lusser, designer of the Messerschmitt M37, worked for the US Navy and the Jet Propulsion Laboratory before joining van Braun's rocketry team; Kurt Debus, former member of both the Nazi Party and the SS, worked on the Apollo programme as director of NASA's Launch Operations Center and was inducted into the National Space Hall of Fame in 1969; Hubertus Strughold, implicated in war crimes committed at Dachau, also worked at NASA and had an award established in his honour by the Space Medicine Association in 1963 for outstanding contributions in space-related medical research; and Bernhard Tessmann lived and worked in Huntsville for the rest of his life.

In fact, only one of the rocket scientists was actually accused of war crimes. Following an investigation into suspected war criminals begun by Eli Rosenbaum in 1979, Arthur Rudolph, manager of the Saturn V programme, recipient of NASA's Distinguished Service Medal and US citizen, agreed to renounce his citizenship and leave the country rather than face Justice

Department charges that he had 'brutalized slave labourers' from the Mittelbau-Dora concentration camp during the war. Rudolph left the US in March 1984 and made his way to West Germany. Although the West German authorities were given evidence by their US counterparts, they declined to prosecute as there was insufficient evidence to justify it.

As a result, Rudolph came to regret his decision and tried to regain his citizenship and return to America. But as part of his agreement to avoid prosecution, he had waived his rights to appeal and to the services of an attorney. He had been uprooted from his retirement home in California and deported. He needed another plan. In 1991, he and his wife took a trip ostensibly to see their daughter in Toronto. However, just as he had planned, they were not allowed to enter the country without a hearing in front of Canadian immigration officials, who had been alerted to his arrival by US officials. At last, he had a platform for airing the evidence for and against his alleged war crimes. He claimed that he was not aware of any mistreatment or the execution of any workers at Nordhausen. However, prosecutors insisted on the fact that he was involved in a mass hanging of workers from a crane situated outside his office. His application for entry to Canada was rejected and he had to leave the country. The story of Rudolph's hearing is told in an unsettling documentary film by Johnny Gogan called *Prisoners of the Moon*, released in 2019.

THE END JUSTIFIES THE MEANS

There can be no doubt that in 1945 and 1946 the prizes on offer from their defeated enemy were too tempting for the Allies to refuse. German science, technology and medical advancements were the envy of the world. As the 1940s drew to a close, so did many of the programmes, and some of those 'kidnapped' to work in Britain, France and the Soviet Union returned home. By that time, the terms of their employment had been sorted out. Many were housed properly and paid, some had lucrative contracts and were joined by their families, and the US was happy to offer citizenship to many of them.

Looking back from a decade after the war, these operations were seen as a success, particularly for the US. In military terms, they already had their rocket programme, they had procured the swept-back single-wing 1944 Horten Ho 229 – arguably the world's first stealth aircraft – acquired the basic knowledge on which to develop Cruise missiles, and learned the best techniques of protecting US soldiers during atomic warfare. Of course, scientists were not the sole targets of these operations. In an effort to deflect criticism of the 'top secret' operation following articles in the press in 1947, President Truman ordered the Department of Commerce to emphasize the more popular advances made with Nazi technology, such as the development of synthetic rubber (used in car tyres), non-running hosiery, the ear thermometer, electromagnetic tape and miniaturized electrical components. They also made advances in producing synthetic fuels, wind tunnel technology, tape recorders, colour film, machine tools, heavy equipment, ceramics, optical glass, dyes and electron microscopes.

For the Russians too, the operation was a success in that the work of the German scientists they captured enabled the Soviet Union to catch up and briefly surpass the US in rocket technology. This happened despite the fact that Stalin had decimated the science research sector during the Great Purge (1936–38), imprisoning or executing the country's top scientists and engineers. If it had not been for German contributions, the Soviets would not have been able to compete in either the arms or space race.

The British were more concerned with commerce, happy to benefit from anything that would give them economic advantages in business and trade, whether that was coal mining, comb making, print technology or the manufacture of perfume. However, they did not ignore military matters. Rocketry, particularly in terms of the V-2 missiles that were used extensively against Britain, was regarded as high priority, particularly in the light of the possibility that one day such a rocket could be fitted with an atomic warhead and change the face of war in the future. Another priority for the British military was chemical warfare. In 1936, IG Farben had developed a nerve agent, tabun, which could inflict great harm on the human nervous system. Further research produced even more potent derivatives, named sarin and soman. The Allies had nothing to compare with the power of such weaponry. British soldiers had stumbled on a truckload of strangely marked shells in a railway marshalling yard near Lübbecke. Investigations were undertaken on the shells, and the documentation discovered with them by scientists at Porton Down in Wiltshire and the devastating effects the use of these new nerve agents would have were revealed. In time, this discovery allowed Britain and the US to add nerve agents to their arsenals.

For France, who shared a 300-mile-long (480 km) border with Germany, collaboration with their former enemies was seen as essential to avoid another damaging conflict between the two countries. As part of their reparations settlement, France occupied the German regions of the Saar and the Ruhr, two of the most productive coalfields in Europe. This was particularly important. Despite its defeat, German industry – in particular its steel production – which operated as a series of cartels to undermine competition, was able to return to pre-war production levels almost immediately. Although the French people were not keen on rapprochement with the newly formed West Germany, the French government knew that agreeing to collaborate on coal might loosen the ties of the steel cartels and break the age-old opposition between the two countries. By 1951, France, Germany, Italy and the Benelux countries had signed the Treaty of Paris. It was the first indication of a European project, created with France and Germany as its major players.

The stories of Operation Paperclip, Osoaviakhim, Alsos, Lusty and others in search of the military, scientific and commercial knowledge of the defeated Nazi regime in Germany followed similar patterns and threw up similar issues. At first, these operations were regarded as 'top secret'. This is not surprising, as they began when the war was still going on, at first in the form of a race not only between the Allies, but one that was focused on preventing the Soviets, by then already identified as the new enemy, from getting their hands on anything that might give them any advantage in the Cold War struggle to come. There were articles in the press about it, but the moral outrage came and went like the previous day's newspapers.

It was only towards the end of the 1970s – American hero Wernher von Braun escaped by the skin of his teeth, dying in 1977 – when the rise of investigative journalism began to reveal the real stories behind these Allied operations, prompting moral outrage that the US and Britain in particular were prepared to smuggle out known war criminals who were responsible for barbarous acts of cruelty, give them new identities, new lives and allow them to avoid accountability for their war crimes. It's true that some very bad men got away with murder. Dr Kurt

Blome, for example, tested the effects of nerve gas on prisoners at Auschwitz. Although arrested and tried at Nuremberg, he was saved from the gallows and whisked off to the US as part of Operation Paperclip. Otto Ambros, Hitler's favourite chemical warfare advisor and co-discoverer of sarin gas, also worked at Auschwitz and was convicted of mass murder and using slave labour at Nuremberg. He was granted clemency and invited to the US to work for the army and Dow Chemical. Dr Herbert Gerstner, who conducted hundreds of experiments on 'feeble-minded children' and the elderly before they were killed in Hitler's T4 euthanasia programme, was recruited under Paperclip to conduct radiation experiments on dying cancer patients in Texas. But it did not seem to matter. Unofficial US policy decided that it was necessary to procure these Nazis to accelerate America's scientific, technological and economic advancement. As von Braun had calculated before he surrendered to the Americans, no matter what atrocities were eventually discovered, no major world power would refuse knowledge of the technological advances made by the Nazis, nor could they afford not to know how to combat them, vaccinate against them or outpace them. Scientific geniuses many of the new citizens may have been, sharing Nobel prizes and other awards between them, and they may all have been more concerned with science than National Socialism, but they were never held accountable for what they did in the war. The understanding then seemed to be that the end always justifies the means: America would benefit a great deal from their input. In moral terms, then, it seems that the peace was almost as costly as the war.

CHAPTER 10

THE LAST NAZIS

IN THE years following World War II, people were consumed with the immediate legacies of conflict. This included dealing with the perceived perpetrators of war crimes through summary justice, through the trials at Nuremberg and elsewhere. But the need for revenge soon diminished, in part because of war fatigue, a general need to move forward and because the West had found a new enemy – the Soviet communists – and was getting involved in Cold War complications. It took at least a generation to reach the necessary distance from the Holocaust to see its full horror and to find the will to confront it. That process began in Jerusalem, the capital of Israel, the still-new nation state of the Jewish people.

THE 'ORDINARY' MAN

On 11 April 1961, the theatre of Beit Ha'am (the House of the People), Jerusalem's newly built cultural centre, was packed with over 700 people for the start of the trial of Adolf Eichmann, architect of the so-called Final Solution – the mass deportation of European Jews to ghettos and extermination camps. The crowd included hundreds of journalists, radio reporters and the American television networks, who were to broadcast proceedings via a live feed to 37 countries, including West Germany. It became the world's first-ever global TV event.

As Eichmann took his place in the courtroom's bulletproof glass booth, the world had its first sight of the small, balding man with thick-rimmed glasses who had been responsible for organizing the systematic murder of six million Jews. For the first time, the world was confronted by the embodiment of Nazi evil. In his ill-fitting suit, laying out his pens and papers and then polishing his glasses, he looked so normal – the personification of what political theorist and author Hannah Arendt, reporting on the trial for the *New Yorker* magazine, called 'the banality of evil'.

In the dock: Nazi war criminal Adolf Eichmann on trial in Jerusalem, 1961.

During the 14-week trial, the court heard evidence from 112 witnesses, many of them survivors of the Holocaust. The prosecution's intention was not only to establish Eichmann's guilt, as no one doubted this, but to present a picture of the Holocaust as a whole, exposing the horrific details to millions for the first time. One of the survivors, Rivka Yosselevska, told the court about her escape from the execution pit at Zagrodzki in Belarus in 1942. On the evening of Friday 14 August, the village ghetto, home to some 500 Jewish families, was surrounded by a detachment of SS *Einsatzgruppen* troops. The following morning, the people were told to line up and remove their clothes. Naked, they were herded towards a pit and shot. Yosselevska watched as the other 11 members of her family were killed, their bodies pushed into the pit below. She, too, was shot in the head, but survived, lying among the bodies for three days and nights before being rescued by a farmer who hid her, fed her and eventually helped her join a group of Jews hiding in a nearby forest. They stayed in hiding until the arrival of the Soviet army in the summer of 1944. Dr Martin Foldi described how he, his wife, son and daughter were taken from Hungary to Auschwitz in a cattle truck. On arrival, two lines were formed: Foldi went right; his wife, son and daughter went left. Foldi had recently bought a red coat for his two-year-old daughter. When he looked up moments after being separated from his family, he could not see his wife and son, but, he said, he could 'see the little red dot getting smaller and smaller – this is how my family disappeared from my life'.

Eichmann listened impassively to a translation of the trial from his glass cubicle, hearing the witnesses' stories. Some of them had actually encountered Eichmann during their captivity and spoke of his 'enthusiasm' and 'fanatical zeal and unquenchable bloodthirst'; others simply told their own stories in tragic detail. In his defence, Eichmann insisted that he was a minor functionary with no choice but to follow orders. A small cog in a big wheel, just a functionary, an ordinary man. He explained that following a decision taken by Hitler and planned at the Wannsee Conference in January 1942, Göring instructed Heydrich to submit a plan for a 'total solution to the Jewish question'. Heydrich and Eichmann were then charged with the task of ensuring that all Jews in German-occupied Europe were to be killed. He felt no guilt for putting the plan into action, and no guilt for the consequences.

The trial finished on 12 August 1961. On 12 December, presentation of the judges' verdict began. Eichmann's defence of 'following orders' was rejected. Although he was found personally not guilty of any killings, he was deemed responsible for procuring Jews for the camps, the terrible transport conditions that took them to their deaths and for being a 'key perpetrator' of the Jewish genocide. He was sentenced to death by hanging. Following unsuccessful appeals, the sentence was carried out on 1 June 1962 at the prison in Ramla. Hours later, his body was cremated and the ashes scattered at sea beyond Israel's territorial waters.

The trial, the story of which is told in detail in the 2015 film *The Eichmann Show*, was a sensation, and the testimony of the survivors heard for the first time by millions of people, Jewish and otherwise, left a powerful legacy. Until then, even in Israel itself, their stories were not believed, little discussed and soon forgotten; survivors were looked down on as though they were in some way complicit in the horrors that had occurred in the concentration and death camps. As the trial gathered pace, however, all the talk in Israeli shops, cafés and markets was of that day's events in the courtroom. As the witnesses spoke, they were actually listened to, and people heard the tragic, heart-rending stories first hand, just as Eichmann was forced to do during the proceedings. The trial finally burst the wall of near silence that had surrounded what the founder and first prime minister of Israel David Ben-Gurion called 'the only crime that has no parallel in human history'.

ON THE HUNT

Even though World War II ended more than 75 years ago, newspapers and news websites are still peppered with stories of the trials of former Nazi camp guards, medical staff and other functionaries – stories printed because of the world's enduring fascination with this horrifying phenomenon.

Nazi hunting began well before the Nazis surrendered in May 1945. That year, the British War Crimes investigation team helped find Rudolf Höss, former commandant at Auschwitz, while the US Counterintelligence Corps, led by Robert E. Matteson, captured Walter Riedel – construction chief of the V-2 rocket programme – and Ernst Kaltenbrunner, head of the Reich Main Security Office. However, these Allied government-run organizations began to run down their operations as early as November 1946, citing lack of personnel, lack of expertise, costs, and so on. In reality, this was more likely to have been a political decision, as complaints against the methods used by British, French and American investigators became more and more frequent.

Nazi hunting, however, did not go away. In the 1950s, Israeli intelligence agency Mossad took up the challenge, locating Eichmann, who was living in Buenos Aires where he worked in the Mercedes-Benz factory under the name Ricardo Klement, kidnapping him and secretly bringing him back to Israel to face justice. It is also alleged that they located Josef Mengele in South America before deciding not to arrest him. Mossad had been informed that Mengele was in Brazil by Simon Wiesenthal, perhaps the most famous of all Nazi hunters. Born to a Jewish family in Austria in 1908, Wiesenthal survived incarceration in 11 different Nazi death camps between 1941 and 1945. Convinced that his survival had a purpose, he made it his life's work to track down and punish the perpetrators of the Holocaust. By the time he died in 2005, his investigations had ferreted out nearly 1,100 Nazi war criminals. The Simon Wiesenthal Center, named in his honour, has published an annual 'most wanted' list of Nazi war criminals since 2001, which is drawn up by Efraim Zuroff, director of the organization's Jerusalem office.

Serge and Beate Klarsfeld have been hunting Nazis for 70 years. Based in Paris, the couple have spent their lives in search of justice for the victims and survivors of SS war crimes in France and of French Vichy collaborators. Serge is Jewish and was born in Romania, but the family migrated to France before the start of World War II. In 1943, his father was sent to Auschwitz, where he died. His German wife, Beate, is not Jewish but pledged to 'dedicate her life to Holocaust victims and survivors' as an 'act of atonement' for the actions of her fellow countrymen.

They have brought at least 10 war criminals and collaborators to justice, including Klaus Barbie (see page 145), who was convicted and sent to prison for life in 1987; former Paris police chief Maurice Papon, who was responsible for the deportation of 140,000 French Jews; and the collaborator René Bousquet, who discovered 44 Jewish children in the village of Izieu in eastern France. They were rounded up and sent to Auschwitz, where they were gassed and burned. With few Nazis left to trace, the Klarsfelds now spend much of their time documenting the Holocaust in France.

The one remaining state department with an interest in Nazi hunting is the Central Office for the Investigation of National Socialist Crimes. Set up by the West German government in 1958, its offices are in Ludwigsburg in south-west Germany. Much of its work involves sifting through the files and other records of former concentration camps in what the staff call 'a giant cold-case operation', but investigators are also often in South America. Inside its offices is an ever-expanding archive of 1.7 million index cards recording the names of massacres, battles, concentration camps, victims, witnesses and perpetrators. It is the world's most comprehensive repository of Nazi crimes and post-war attempts to bring the regime to justice. In 2016, it launched an operation in Brazil when a German police detective, Uwe Steinz, was charged with searching the national archives in Rio for immigration records. He returned empty-handed. With any remaining Nazis now sure to be in their 90s and likely to have been low-level functionaries, it seems probable that the department will soon be closed forever.

Of course, over the years some searches were more successful than others.

THE MENGELE MYSTERY

One day in early February 1979, Josef Mengele and his friends, the Bosserts, went to the beach at Bertioga near São Paulo in Brazil. It was a hot day and the Atlantic waters were calm and cooling. At some point during the afternoon, the bad-tempered and overheated Mengele went for a swim. Some ten minutes later, he suffered a stroke that paralysed one side of his body.

He struggled for his life, but when rescuers reached him he was dead. His body was pulled on to the beach, where it lay until the police arrived later that evening.

Mengele was buried on a hillside in Embu das Artes, to the west of the city in which had a lived, with little ceremony under the name Wolfgang Gerhard, based on the identity card he had been carrying during his trip to the beach. Mengele's family kept his death a secret to protect those who had offered him shelter during his years on the run.

The mystery began to unravel in 1985. Simon Wiesenthal claimed that there had been several sightings in Greece, in Egypt and in Spain during the 1960s and 1970s, but he was not found. In February 1985, a mock trial was held in Jerusalem that heard witness statements from over a hundred victims of Mengele's medical experiments, and worldwide interest in his whereabouts intensified when rewards were offered for his capture. Acting on information received from West German authorities, the police raided the home of his lifelong friend, Hans Sedlmeier, who was also sales manager for the Mengele family firm in Günzburg. Among the papers, they found a letter from Wolfram Bossert informing Sedlmeier of Mengele's death in 1979. The Bosserts were then arrested by Brazilian police. They informed the police of the location of Mengele's grave and his body was exhumed for identification, which proved positive.

The story was fleshed out by journalist John Ware in an article published in the *Jewish Chronicle* in February 2020. Ware had conducted his own hunt for Mengele in 1978, while researching an edition of ITV's *World in Action*. Needless to say, he did not locate the missing Nazi. However, in 1985, while researching material for a biography of Mengele, he interviewed the doctor's only son, Rolf. Born in 1944, Rolf stayed in Germany with his mother when his father fled the country for Argentina in 1949. The couple divorced in 1954. Rolf only met his father twice, once in Switzerland in 1956 – although he was told at the time that this was his Uncle Fritz – and again in 1977, when Rolf travelled to Brazil in secret to find out the truth about the horrific allegations against his own flesh and blood that had blighted his life.

Over the course of the two-week visit, Mengele revealed the secrets of his life as a fugitive in South America, his fears when Eichmann was arrested and tried, his bitterness, his depression, his sleeplessness and his nightmares. But he was unrepentant about what he had done during the war. He said that he had 'not invented Auschwitz', that his selections 'on the ramp' had saved those still able to work, and that he 'had to do his duty, to carry out orders'. It was their last meeting.

Following the discovery of his father's grave in 1985, Rolf explained why Mengele's death had been kept secret. He also agreed to the publication of excerpts from a number of the diaries his father had kept during his lifetime. In 1992, DNA testing confirmed the identity of Mengele's bones and the mystery was finally laid to rest. Today, the skeleton is used during forensic medicine courses at the University of São Paulo's medical school, connecting his bones to the life story of the man they called the 'Angel of Death'.

THE HONORARY DOCTOR

In the summer of 2000, a benign, elderly lady was enjoying her extensive rose garden overlooking the Thuringian city of Jena and the wide valley of the River Saale. The garden, and the very comfortable bourgeois house that it surrounded, were rewards for outstanding service as a functionary of the German Democratic Republic. Dr Rosemarie Albrecht had retired many years before in 1975, and been showered with compliments and gifts that reflected her position as a much-respected dean of the medical faculty at the local university and one of the leading scientists in the GDR. Her early research had investigated the chemical qualities of breast milk, but her most significant work had been her collaboration with the optics company ZEISS Jena, developing the use of microscopic technologies in diagnosing cancerous malignancies. It had won her the ultimate title of Honorary Doctor of the People. Now, in her 84th year, the reputation of this medical pioneer was in danger of evaporating. A light had unexpectedly been shone on events that took place in a hospital almost 60 years before in an entirely different Germany.

In 2000, a long-forgotten collection of documents was rediscovered in the archives of the now defunct GDR. The documents had been created in Nazi Germany and then ignored in communist times. They had gathered dust throughout five decades, when prosecutors in the two post-war Germanies had little appetite for raking up inconvenient problems from the past. But with the beginning of the new century, the age of collective amnesia was over and there was an urgent desire to hunt down and punish the last agents of Hitler's Reich before they inevitably passed away. In 2003, the materials in the archive were made available to the families of victims and to accredited historians. The documents suggested that more than 200,000 'useless people' had been killed in Nazi euthanasia programmes within the provinces that had comprised the Soviet sector and then East Germany. Some victims had been sent to the gas chambers; many had been murdered by drug overdose or had simply been left to die from neglect. Among the files were folders of papers and notes meticulously recording the activities at a psychiatric hospital in the small town of Stadtroda, 10 miles (16 km) east of Jena. Having completed her studies, the 26-year-old Rosemarie Albrecht began her medical career there, first as a voluntary assistant and then as the doctor in charge of the women's ward. Over 900 patients were murdered at the Stadtroda hospital, and Dr Albrecht's name was said to be connected to the deaths of 159 women. Her name was linked to the death of a 34-year-old woman diagnosed as 'schizophrenic with debility'. The patient died on 20 April (Hitler's birthday) in 1941 as a result of a lethal cocktail of sleeping pills, including Evipan, Luminal, Pernocton and Veronal. One document that seemed to have been written or at least signed off by her described 11 handicapped children as 'waste material'. All 11 died in her 'care'. She was implicated by another record, which referred to a child being murdered for reasons of 'hereditary hygiene'. And there was the death of Helene Fleischer, a local communist politician who had been in the Nazi prison system since 1934. Labelled as schizophrenic and suffering from tuberculosis, Fleischer ended up in Albrecht's ward at Stadtroda, where she was murdered in June 1941.

In February 2004, Albrecht was charged with the murder of the 34-year-old woman, but the process of bringing a viable prosecution was soon bogged down. There were no living witnesses to the events that led to the patient's death, and the surviving documentation was ambiguous. It was alleged that the patient concerned had been deliberately starved, but the ward notes stated that the patient had repeatedly refused food that was offered to her. Albrecht was charged with death by overdose, but several experts pointed out that the dosages she administered were within the normal limits indicated in medical textbooks published in the 1920s and 1930s, and within the prescription limit still being advised in several European countries well into the 1950s. A 103-year-old doctor was found who remembered Albrecht as a young friendly colleague who was dedicated to her calling. A petition of 22 local doctors offered her support, as did senior figures in the State Medical Association. As the date of the trial approached, a more nuanced picture of Albrecht had emerged that was increasingly at odds with the image of the evil mass murderer on the posters of the anti-Nazi protesters on the streets of Jena. Albrecht's folksy but pugnacious defence of her innocence in front of the cameras won over many television viewers. Her case dominated the media across Germany: pundits on the chat shows discussed not just her innocence or guilt, but argued as much about the value and purpose of prosecuting this one aged individual rather than holding the entire medical culture of the times to account. Some argued that Albrecht's real crime was to have outlived the decades when the subject of Nazi euthanasia had been conveniently ignored; she was being brought to a symbolic trial because there was virtually no else left from that dark period in German medical history. A few weeks before her 90th birthday in March 2005, Albrecht's doctors judged that she was no longer fit enough to stand trial. The court officers were relieved; they had already stated that she would almost certainly have been acquitted due to lack of evidence. When Dr Rosemarie Albrecht died in 2008, some remembered an outstanding medical practitioner and researcher who made a significant contribution to medical progress; others thought of her as a murderer who had carried out Nazi orders either willingly or at least without protest. She was, of course, both of these people.

OPERATION LAST CHANCE

In 2008, Efraim Zuroff, of the Simon Wiesenthal Center in Los Angeles, launched Operation Last Chance, aimed at bringing the remaining Nazis to justice. He said: 'During the past 15 years, at least 103 convictions against Nazi war criminals have been obtained, at least 102 new indictments have been filed, and well over 3,600 new investigations have been initiated. Despite the somewhat prevalent assumption that it is too late to bring Nazi murderers to justice, the figures clearly prove otherwise, and we are trying to ensure that at least several of these criminals will be brought to trial during the coming years. While it is generally assumed that it is the age of the suspects that is the biggest obstacle to prosecution, in many cases it is the lack of political will, more than anything else, that has hindered the efforts to bring Holocaust perpetrators to justice.'

One of the operation's most famous cases was using accessory to murder charges against Sobibor death camp guard Ivan Demjanjuk in 2011. Ukrainian by birth, former farm worker Demjanjuk was serving in the Red Army when he was captured by the Wehrmacht in 1942 after the Battle of Kerch in the Crimean peninsula. He took the option of serving as a volunteer auxiliary death camp guard for the SS rather than remain as a Soviet 'guest' in Chelm POW camp in Poland. He was trained for his duties at Trawniki between July and September 1942 before serving at various camps.

Finally freed from captivity in Germany after the war, he and his family emigrated to the United States, settling in a suburb of Cleveland, Ohio, and working at the local Ford Motors plant. He was awarded US citizenship under the name John Demjanjuk in 1958. In 1977, press articles – using evidence based on an identity card found in Ukraine – indicated that he

Perhaps the most famous Nazi hunter of all, Simon Wiesenthal displays photographs depicting former Gestapo chief Walter Rauff, then living openly in Santiago, Chile, and an ambulance used to execute Jews. Wiesenthal was asking President Ronald Reagan to use his influence to help extricate accused Nazi war criminals living in South America.

was in fact Ivan the Terrible, a sadistic guard who ran the gas chambers at the Treblinka death camp in Nazi-occupied Poland, where an estimated 800,000 prisoners were murdered. In 1983, US officials stripped him of his citizenship and extradited him to Israel on account of the false information he had given on his arrival in America back in 1952. He was to face trial for war crimes and crimes against humanity.

During the trial, again held in Jerusalem, Demjanjuk claimed that he had been a POW at Chelm throughout the period 1942 to 1944, and therefore could not have been at Treblinka. However, his story was contradicted by five survivors of the Polish death camp who readily identified him as Ivan the Terrible. One witness, Eliahu Rosenberg, approached the prisoner and asked him to remove his glasses. Returning to the witness box, he declared, 'This is Ivan. I say so unhesitatingly and without the slightest doubt. Ivan from Treblinka. The man I am looking at now. I saw those eyes, those murderous eyes.' Based on this evidence, the judges had little choice but to agree that he was Ivan the Terrible, and found him guilty of all charges. He was sentenced to death by hanging and put in solitary confinement while the scaffold was built.

After a lengthy appeals process, Demjanjuk was acquitted following written statements by 37 former guards at Treblinka saying that Ivan the Terrible was another Ukrainian, Ivan Marchenko. In 1998, having spent seven years in an Israeli prison, Demjanjuk returned to the US and had his citizenship restored following allegations that the US authorities had hidden evidence of his real identity from the Israeli court. However, in 2001 more charges were brought against him, this time for complicity in the deaths of almost 30,000 Jews at Sobibor and Majdanek, and of membership of an SS Death's Head battalion at Flossenbürg. Denied an appeal, he was deported to Germany in 2009 to face another trial.

By then, despite being 89 years old and suffering from a number of health issues, he was deemed fit to take part in the trial in Munich. Most of the evidence heard offered detailed descriptions of the horrors that took place in the camp, but no one was able to identify him as a guard there. Two years later, Demjanjuk was convicted as an accessory to the murder of 27,900 Jews at Sobibor. He was given a five-year sentence with two years already served. Released from custody pending an appeal, he died in an old people's home in 2012.

Despite the guilty verdict, because he died with his case pending appeal, he was 'presumed innocent' under German law. Nonetheless, his conviction – only on the basis of having been a guard at a death camp – set a new legal precedent. Before this, prosecution had to be on the basis of a specific act or acts of murder, which had resulted in low prosecution rates for camp guards and others involved in the industrial nature of Nazi war killings. Following this verdict, a number of new cases were brought against former death camp guards, such as Oskar Gröning, as well those who worked at concentration camps, including Johann Rehbogen, Reinhold Hanning and Bruno Dey (see page 242).

THE 'PREGNANT MONSTER'

Erna Pfannstiel was born in 1922 in eastern Germany and raised by her postal clerk father. She joined the Nazi Party aged 19 and was trained to be a concentration camp guard. She first served at Ravensbrück before being transferred to Majdanek, near Lublin in Poland, in 1942. There was significant witness evidence that Erna was a sadistic guard who volunteered and enjoyed selection duties 'on the ramp'. She was said to have beaten, goaded and mocked victims, and was reported to have laughed at victims en route to the gas chambers. She was also accused by several witnesses of having beaten a young Jewish boy to death.

During her time at Majdanek, she met and married a fellow guard, Georg Wallisch. She was soon pregnant, and was later known by some inmates as the 'pregnant monster' because of her brutal behaviour. In late 1944, George was arrested for stealing Reich property, namely gold watches taken from Jews arriving at the camp. He was sentenced to three years in prison and was interned by the Russians when they liberated the camp the following year.

When the war ended, Erna Wallisch and her daughter moved to Vienna, living in a small apartment in the Kaisermühlen district overlooking the Danube. She lived freely and without guilt, with her name on the doorbell of the apartment. Neighbours described her as friendly, helpful and pleasant, many sharing the common attitudes of post-war Austria that the war was 'all in the past, people should learn to forgive'.

Easy to track down by researchers, journalists and prosecutors, she remained of recurring interest to the Austrian authorities. She was investigated at Graz in 1965, but charges were dismissed due to insufficient evidence. Pressure rose again in the early 1970s, but investigations described her complicity in the killings at Majdanek as merely *entfernte Schuld* – 'distant guilt'. The authorities ruled that she was 'a possible participant in sadistic activities but not a perpetrator'. The charges were finally dropped as the Austrian statutes of limitation had expired.

In 2007, after continued pressure from Efraim Zuroff at the Simon Wiesenthal Center, who had identified five Polish witnesses from Majdanek who were prepared to offer evidence against her, the Austrian authorities began preparing a case. However, the 86-year-old Wallisch died in a hospital bed in February 2008 and the case was closed.

Despite Austrian newspaper reports that the authorities had acted as if they had 'no desire to arouse the demons of the past', and accusing them of stalling in the hope that her poor health and death would absolve them of the need to take action, Erma Wallisch was never called to account for her actions.

GENOCIDE – A FAMILY TRADITION

In February 1999, 72-year-old Nada Šakić was released from prison in Croatia and exonerated for crimes of cruelty and mass murder committed while she was commander of Stara Gradiška, a subcamp of the Jasenovac death camp complex during World War II. She had been extradited from Argentina the previous year. Interrogated by Croatian officials in Zagreb, she was released due to 'lack of sufficient evidence', which, according to the judge, had been 'thin' and 'poorly remembered' by the elderly witnesses.

Genocide was a family profession for Nada Luburić, who was born in 1926. Connected to key families in the Ustaše, she was the half-sister of an important general, Maks Luburić, the first commander at Jasenovac, and wife of Dinko Šakić, who succeeded Luburić at the notorious camp. She also 'worked' there, nominally as a guard, although she was accused of participating in torture and mass killings during her time there.

Stara Gradiška was specially constructed by the Ustaše as an extermination camp for women and children of Serb, Jewish, Gypsy, Croat and Bosnian ethnicity. Inmates were systematically murdered by various means: torture, crushing skulls with heavy hammers, shooting, stabbing, strangling with piano wire, the Serbian throat-slitter, starvation and gassed in vans with Zyklon B. It is estimated that at least 6,000 victims were killed when Nada and Dinko were known to be active there. In a camp known for the barbaric cruelty of the staff, survivors agreed that the worst offender was Nada Luburić.

Nada and Dinko Šakić were married in 1943. Following the war, they fled Croatia via Spain to Argentina. Arriving in 1947, they were welcomed by Juan Perón. Nada changed her name to Esperanza, and the couple settled in a small village called Santa Teresita on the coast near Buenos Aires. They started up a number of textile and fashion export companies, enjoying life for almost 50 years without the need to hide their identities, as part of a large Croat community.

In 1997, agents at the Simon Wiesenthal Center tracked the pair down, and in the resultant publicity TV executives in Argentina asked Dinko for an interview, ostensibly to discuss Croatia as Argentina's opponents in the upcoming World Cup, to which he agreed. The interview, aired in March 1998, was a disaster for Dinko, when he confirmed his role as commander at what had become known as World War II's most notorious death camp. Despite his claim that during his time no one was tortured or killed at Jasenovac, 'they just all died from disease', the damage had been done. Uproar followed the interview and Argentina's president Carlos Menem called for his arrest, which followed on 1 May. He was extradited to Croatia for his trial on charges of genocide, even though Serbia had requested that it be held in Belgrade. Nada's extradition followed in November 1998, a month before the start of the trial. Video exists of the arrival at Zagreb of a frail old lady, apparently suffering from advanced Parkinson's, who had the made the long journey 'to explain and clarify her role in the history of wartime Croatia', according to her lawyer.

In the event, Dinko Šakić was charged with crimes against civilians and accused of personally carrying out executions during his time at Jasenovac in 1944. He was unrepentant. While he was found guilty and sentenced to the maximum 20 years in prison, it was seen by many as window dressing when news leaked out that he had a comfortable cell, complete with TV, a computer provided for him to write his memoirs, and regular visits from his wife. Dinko spent the last decade of his life dogged by heart disease and long periods in hospital. He died in July 2008 and was cremated in his full Ustaše uniform. Serbia issued an arrest warrant for his wife Nada in July 2011, but the Croatian media reported that she had died in February that year at the age of 85.

The way that Dinko and Nada were dealt with after extradition, with soft, lenient sentences, semi-heroic references in the Croatia media and a popular willingness to forget and excuse their wartime atrocities, is taken as evidence of the enduring tribal loyalties and rivalries that exist in the Balkans to this day.

YOUR NEIGHBOUR IS A NAZI

During the 2000s, the streets of Queens, a borough of New York City, often resounded to the sounds of protests outside a regular red-brick, two-storey house, as outraged members of the local Jewish community struck up the chant, 'your neighbour is a Nazi'. The target of their ire was Jakiw Palij, who lived in quiet retirement with his wife in Jackson Heights.

Born in Poland in an area that is now part of Ukraine, he had first arrived in Boston in 1949, via one of the established ratlines.

Armed with false papers, he told US immigration officers that he had been excused military service in the war because of his essential work on his family farm and then in factories when his land had been swallowed up by the Soviets. He was allowed to enter the country as a DP and granted American citizenship in 1957. He trained and worked as a draughtsman, got married in 1960 and retired to his house in Queens in 1966. Neighbours remembered him as a very reserved, polite, quiet man.

His peace was shattered in 1993 when investigators rang on his bell, having been alerted to his past by a former colleague who had worked with him at Trawniki labour camp in German-occupied Poland. He was interviewed by US investigative authorities and admitted that he had been a security guard at the camp and had lied about it to immigration officials when he first arrived in America. 'I lied, everyone lied, I would never have got a visa if I had told the truth,' he said. He denied any involvement in war crimes, saying that he worked at the camp, 'only because my family was threatened by the SS'. Investigations revealed very little about his actual service in German units, other than his training at Trawniki and some evidence of guarding Jewish prisoners there. He was briefly promoted to the rank of *Oberwachmann*, and was probably involved in organizing civilian units in Poland and Prussia in digging trenches and building ramparts and tank traps for the Wehrmacht in 1944–45.

In 2001, the US Department of Justice tried again, revealing that Palij had performed the usual perimeter guard duties, but also that he had been a member of the Streibel SS battalion, a unit that committed inhuman crimes and atrocities against Polish citizens and others, and that he was also involved in cremating the remains of camp victims and Wehrmacht dead on the Eastern Front. It also alleged that he was involved in the massacre of 6,000 inmates at the camp in November 1943, part of Operation Reinhard, the Third Reich's plan to murder Jews in Poland. Palij denied the allegations.

In 2003, his US citizenship was revoked for 'participation in acts against Jewish citizens', and the authorities attempted to arrange his deportation. However, as he was officially stateless, Poland, Ukraine and Germany all refused to take him. His continued presence in the US prompted the local demonstrations organized by anti-Holocaust groups and local Jewish schools. Under pressure from this and sustained press and media attention, the Senate and the House persuaded the State Department to open US–German negotiations once more about a possible deportation. Despite the fact that his alleged crimes happened outside Germany and that the prosecutors had no evidence to justify trial proceedings, Germany agreed to take him as part of a collaborative effort between the US and a key European ally.

In August 2018, the 95-year-old former concentration camp guard arrived in Düsseldorf and was taken to a care home in Ahlen, near Munster. Although plans were made to try him using the Demjanjuk ruling of accessory to murder, he died in January 2019 before the trial could take place.

THE LAST NAZI?

On 17 October 2019, what is likely to be one of the last Nazi trials began in Hamburg. Bruno Dey, a member of the SS's Death's Head battalion and a tower guard at the concentration camp at Stutthof, near modern-day Gdańsk in Poland, between August 1944 and April 1945, was accused of being an accessory to 5,230 deaths. Stutthof housed mostly Jews from the Baltic states, as well as some overspill from Auschwitz, 5,000 of whom had died from hunger, typhus and lack of medical care, having been forced to live in unhygienic conditions that encouraged disease, while 200 had been gassed with Zyklon B, and 30 shot.

Prosecutors had found Dey's name on a list of surviving guards at Stutthof discovered in the camp's museum, which also gave details of his rota hours. His task was mainly to prevent any inmates escaping. As Dey was technically a minor, aged 17 at the time he served in the camp, he was tried under the conditions of a court for youth offenders. Dey was 93 years old when the trial started.

Prosecutors did not offer any direct evidence that Dey had killed or even mistreated anyone, but followed the post-Demjanjuk argument that he had been a cog in the killing machine, and that by the willing performance of his duties, especially stopping prisoners from escaping, he had contributed to many deaths. They also claimed that he had the opportunity of leaving the camp system by returning to the Wehrmacht and reporting for combat duties, a course followed by thousands of other camp guards – the SS did not want the faint-hearted and the uncommitted in the camps. But Dey claimed that he was unfit for combat due to a heart defect, hence he was put to camp guarding in the first place against his will. He also said he feared he might be punished by the SS for asking to be transferred out.

Twenty witnesses appeared, all Holocaust survivors but not all from Stutthof, and none of whom could identify Dey with any certainly. They described general events at various camps and their own personal experience. Like most post-Demjanjuk trials, process was a symbolic, historic act rather than a trial over specific offences, a fact made clear by the final witness who remarked that it was not so much the individual Dey who was on trial, but the entire Nazi programme of the Holocaust.

In his defence, Dey claimed he was innocent of the charges because he was not directly involved in the killings and was mostly directed to general guarding, perimeter wire and watchtower duties. He also claimed that he did not know the extent of the atrocities at Stutthof, and did not fire a shot during his time there. He stressed that he worked on the perimeter of the camp, well away from the killings. Dey admitted that he heard screams and other sounds of terrified people and assumed that people were being punished in some way, possibly killed, but said that he didn't see this. He also claimed that he did not know that the prisoners were Jews; he assumed some of them were, but that others were simply enemies of the state. When prosecutors produced photographs that showed watchtowers close to the gas chambers, Dey admitted hearing the screams of the victims and seeing bodies being carted away from the camp, and that he had been haunted by those images throughout his subsequent life.

Towards the end of the trial, Dey insisted that he was forced to serve in the camp, but then issued an apology, saying, 'The witness testimony and the expert assessments have made me realize the full scope of the horrors and suffering... Today I would like to apologize to those who went through this hell of madness, and their relatives – something like this can never be repeated.' As part of his closing argument, Dey's lawyer, who had argued for his client to be acquitted because of his unimportance in the camp system, said, 'How could an 18-year-old step out of line in a place like Stutthof?'

On 23 July 2020, Dey was found guilty of the charges and given a two-year suspended sentence. Addressing Dey during the verdict, judge Anne Meier-Göring said, 'The concentration camp Stutthof and the mass murder that took place inside was only possible with your help.'

It is very likely that the Dey process will be the last Nazi trial. As of August 2020, German authorities had 13 outstanding cases that involved a surviving Holocaust participant. All are in their late 90s or older, and it must be shown that they have the physical and mental strength to 'negotiate' a court process – in Dey's case, court sessions were strictly limited to two hours per day, as that was deemed the maximum he could cope with. Most of the remaining possible defendants are older than Dey.

In 2020, the top three remaining Nazi war criminals were all members of *Einsatzgruppen C*, a mobile killing squad whose mission was to exterminate Jews in captured territories. Kurt Gosdek (98), Herbert Walther (99) and Wilhelm Karl Friedrich Hoffmeister (97) were all members of a unit responsible for the mass killings at Babi Yar in the Ukraine in September 1941 (see page 77). The three were tracked down and reported to the German authorities – they are all are said to live in Germany – by Efraim Zuroff, director of the Simon Wiesenthal Center in Jerusalem. There is no news of the investigations, but time is running out...

AFTERWORD

HISTORY RECALLS that the guns fell silent at 23:01 on 8 May 1945, a silence further deepened by the apparent and sudden disappearance of Nazis from all levels of the Party. Of course, many had already left the country. With the gradual realization that Germany would lose the war, high-ranking Nazis, knowing that their complicity in Hitler's murderous regime would result in the harshest justice, began planning their escape routes. That planning turned into action during the last months of the war. Others, lower down the chain of command, hastily took down the portraits of Hitler from their mantelpieces, burned their Hitler Youth uniforms or SA ration books, and prepared to return to their normal lives.

In the immediate aftermath of the conflict, international opinion held that Germany was guilty and justice had to be seen to be done. With Nazism's deep roots – 8.5 million party members and 18 million soldiers, with almost everyone involved either by consent or coercion – the Allies faced a difficult question, 'How do you punish a whole society for its crimes?' In the early months of the Allied occupation, several hundred thousand former Nazis were 'automatically arrested' and interned according to the *Arrest Categories Handbook* that had been issued in April 1945. Allied forces had also arrived in Germany armed with 'Black Lists' of those Nazis of particular interest. Arrests of the latter, normally senior-ranking Nazis, proved popular with the majority of the population, but the targeting of lower-ranking functionaries was a different matter, often leaving civilians unsure of the Allies' motives.

November 1945 saw the first of the Nuremberg Trials, in which the 24 highest-ranking Nazis in captivity were tried by the Allies for war crimes. Although they all pleaded *nicht schuldig* (not guilty) to the charges, 12 of the accused were sentenced to death by hanging – it was a start, even if only a symbolic one. Between 1946 and 1949, there were dozens of other trials in which it is estimated some 50,000 people were convicted.

Meanwhile, behind the scenes, the ratlines and the ratmasters were working at full throttle, providing money, travel documents and tickets to freedom. Escaping Nazis had no shortage of help, from the International Red Cross, the Catholic Church, countries keen to welcome the money and expertise they brought with them, those worried by the threat of communism or those who simply had a grudge against the Allies. Hundreds of thousands – many of them guilty of hideous crimes – poured over the border into Italy and onwards to Europe, South America and elsewhere in search of new lives. Although they are impossible to verify, the numbers were astonishing: some 10,000 were said to have escaped to South America, particularly Argentina, with tens of thousands of others settling in Europe, Asia, North Africa and the Middle East.

Even more extraordinary was that the Allies were exploiting the ratlines for their own purposes, extracting Nazis whose knowledge was of particular interest to them. It became a race as to who got the best brains on offer. As time was of the essence, secret operations were organized to 'recruit' the top scientists, technicians, military designers and chemists. In this way, thousands more Nazis, good and bad, made it out. The moral dilemma of recruiting war criminals was brushed aside, as Allied governments decided 'the end justified the means' – although they still kept their operations secret. It is claimed that in the post-war era there were as many as 10,000 Nazis living in the US.

As time passed, pragmatism prevailed. As well as embarking on a systematic denazification of Germany, the Allies were aware of the need to restart German society, so that even if they had been members of the Nazi Party, ordinary citizens were allowed to return to their jobs as lawyers, teachers, doctors and the like, offering a route back to stability and prosperity. By 1949, international concern about the Cold War had replaced interest in achieving justice for the crimes of World War II – the world simply wanted to move on.

In Germany, the 1950s saw a huge reduction in the prosecution of war crimes and many of those already imprisoned; historian Norbert Frei estimated that up to 800,000 benefited from amnesty laws, which saw them freed from prisons and rehabilitated, returning to their comfortable posts in the judiciary, police and state administration – in many cases, because the presiding officials were former Nazis themselves. But there was much good work done, too. As time began to heal the wounds of guilt, German society adopted a process of *Vergangenheitsbewältigung* (overcoming the past), which forced its citizens to confront not only the evil of Hitler but also the collective responsibility they all bore for the atrocities committed during World War II.

Since the 1960s, the world has remained fascinated by the Nazi era, stimulated for each new generation by events such as the Eichmann trial in 1961, the Mengele story in the 1980s, the 1994 discovery in Rome's Palazzo Cesi of files documenting atrocities in Italy and the Balkans, and the unsealing and immediate resealing in March 2020 – because of COVID-19! – of the Vatican's secret World War II-era files on Pope Pius XII, whose complicity with the Nazis is still contentious. As a consequence, the fundamental questions of whether justice has been done, and 'if not, why not?', remain as unanswered today as they have been since 1945.

In practical terms, punishing every war crime has never been an option. Given that the Central Office for the Investigation of National Socialist Crimes houses an ever-expanding archive of 1.7 million yellow and green index cards recording the names of massacres, battles, concentration camps, victims, witnesses and perpetrators of crimes committed during World War II, the numbers could never add up.

Although figures in the Nazi leadership were by and large punished, either by killing themselves or by the courts, as historian Mary Fulbrook estimates, 'the vast majority of perpetrators got away with it', many of them middle-ranking Nazis who worked in the concentration camp system. In moral terms, the blame for this must be shared with the Allied authorities, who were prepared to look the other way when it came to using Nazi skills and ingenuity for the Cold War fight against communism.

BIBLIOGRAPHY AND OTHER SOURCES

Bessel, Richard, *Germany 1945: From War to Peace* (Simon & Schuster, 2009).

Evans, Harold, *Front Page History: Events of Our Century that Shook the World* (Quiller Press, 1984).

Evans, Richard J., *The Coming of the Third Reich* (Penguin/ Allen Lane, 2004).

Feig, Konnilyn, *Hitler's Death Camps: The Sanity of Madness* (Holmes & Meier, 1981).

Fulbrook, Mary, *Reckonings: Legacies of Nazi Persecution and the Quest for Justice* (OUP, 2018).

Hitler, Adolf, *Mein Kampf* (Vintage 1992, first published in two volumes in 1925–26 by Franz Eher Nachfolger).

Hodgson, Godfrey, *The People's Century: From the Dawn of the Century to the Start of the Cold War* (BBC Books, 1995).

Huber, Florian, *Promise Me You'll Shoot Yourself: The Downfall of Ordinary Germans in 1945* (Allen Lane, 2019).

Kershaw, Ian, *Hitler: 1889–1936 Hubris* (Penguin, 1998).

Kershaw, Ian, *The End: Germany 1944–45* (Penguin, 2011).

Nyiszli, Miklos, *I Was Doctor Mengele's Assistant: The Memoirs of an Auschwitz Physician* (Frap Books, 2010).

Rees, Laurence, *Auschwitz: A New History* (BBC Books, 2005).

Russell, Lord of Liverpool, *The Scourge of the Swastika: A Short History of Nazi War Crimes* (Cassell, 1954).

Shirer, William L, *The Rise and Fall of the Third Reich* (Penguin/ Random House 1998, first published by Secker & Warberg 1960).

Stone, Dan, *The Liberation of the Camps: The End of the Holocaust and Its Aftermath* (Yale University Press, 2015).

There are also a huge number of websites dedicated to World War II. They vary in quality but readers will be rewarded for their diligence and commitment in finding those that feature writing of the finest quality. Below are some recommendations: www.cia.gov; www.eyewitnesstohistory.com; www.famoustrials.com (Nuremberg); www.history.com; www.historyextra.com; www.historytoday; The Holocaust Encyclopedia (www.encyclopedia.ushmm.org); www.theholocaustexplained.org; Institute for Policy Studies (www.ips-dc.org); www.iwm.org.uk; www.jewishvirtuallibrary.org; www.nasa.gov; www.reuters.com; www.tandfonline.com; warfarehistory.com; en-wikipedia.org; www.yadvashem.org

Also useful were the archives of newspapers and magazines including: *The Daily Mail, The Guardian, The Independent, The New York Times, Smithsonian Magazine, TIME* magazine and *The Times of Israel.*

INDEX